How Long Will The Pain Last?

Every Bereaved Parent Wants To Know—

Charlene Cole, M.S.

i

Original painting for cover design by Joyce Runyan

Published In

The United States of America

**In Loving Memory of Joe
&
All of Our Children.
We'll love you as long as we live.**

Foreword

The death of my only child, Joe, started me on a quest to help other bereaved parents, though I had no intention of writing a book at that time. It's been a long journey. My road has been pitted with seemingly insurmountable obstacles – guilt, anger, fear, and depression – to name only a few.

Good help was hard to find. My first psychologist had no clue how to help a bereaved parent, so I tried another. Same result. I read every book I could find on grief, and some did help. Those written by or for bereaved parents were the most helpful. My friends were sure that religious books would help. They didn't. Finally, I found The Compassionate Friends, a support group for bereaved parents, and they understood.

Because I had experienced such a difficult time finding help, I went back to school to get a Masters Degree in Counseling Psychology, hoping to help others along their path. While working on my thesis about parental bereavement, I was given permission to give out anonymous surveys at both The National Compassionate Friends Convention and the National Alive Alone Convention (for parents with no remaining children). To my amazement, the bereaved parents poured out their troubled hearts in these surveys. Their answers to the questions are so poignant that I feel I have to share some of them with you. These quotes helped me, and I think they will help you too.

Purpose of *How Long Will the Pain Last?*

The most important purpose of my book is to give you hope. At first, there seemed to be none for me. After my son's death, I truly believed that my life was over, and the rest of my life would be lived in unbearable pain. My hopes and dreams for the future were shattered, so how could I possibly be happy again? While it is true that happiness *as I knew it* was gone, I eventually discovered that happiness entered my life in *new* ways. Your struggle to find happiness will be unique and different than mine, but you **will** find happiness again, though it may not seem like a possibility at this time. You and I have exited the doorway to our cherished past, but we have entered a new realm. We can have new beginnings and dream new dreams. The sun will shine again.

Many tips and techniques are given to help you deal with special emotions and issues. Some may help you, some may not. Grief is as individual as a fingerprint.

Therapists, clergy, family and friends will also benefit from reading this book. The depth of our pain is usually unfathomable to others, so reading this book will help them better understand how to help us.

Table of Contents

Chapter 1

Our Story
My Son and I

Labor Day weekend was coming up, and I decided to go to Dallas to pick up a new little collie puppy from my cousin, Sandy. The crisp autumn days and colorful leaves of fall were exceptional that September, 1985, so I looked forward to seeing the beautiful foliage along the way. However, I knew I should not go. I had

a strong feeling that something would go terribly wrong, but I did go because my elderly aunt would be disappointed if I did not. What could go wrong? I told myself that I would be extra careful driving.

I arrived safely and all seemed well. Was I apprehen-

Joe and his girlfriend Sara

Joe, age 7

Joe on family vacation

1

sive for nothing? Probably. Aunt Lillie had prepared one of our favorite meals - roast beef with mushroom gravy- and as we talked, laughed, and shared a great meal, my earlier fears vanished. I went to bed thinking, *See, you worried for nothing. Everything's okay.* Little did I know that in a few short hours, my life as I knew it would be over.

Early the next morning, I awoke with a start, knowing that something was tragically wrong. I also knew that it had to do with my nineteen-year-old son, Joe, my only child. I tried to rationalize. Joe was going through a difficult age and I worried anyway, so might these feelings just be an extension of my continual worry? Gene, my husband and Joe's stepfather, would certainly call if something was wrong. Wouldn't he?

About 9:00 A.M., my cousin brought my new little fluffy puppy to me. She also brought terrible news. Almost as soon as she arrived, she handed me the puppy and said, "Betty, hold your puppy tight, because you're going to need its love and comfort."

I'm sure I looked at her quizzically but with dread. "What are you talking about?" I asked but did not want to know.

Sandy then gave me the news that crumbled my world into tiny pieces: "Betty, your son Joe is dead." I heard her words, but I remember feeling nothing. I thought, *How can this be? She just told me that Joe, my precious child, is dead, and I feel nothing?* Of course, I now realize that I was in shock, and for that, I'm so grateful. I do not believe our systems can stand the sudden rush of trauma otherwise.

When I talked with my husband Gene, I asked, "Why didn't you call me?"

He was crying when he answered, "I could not stand for you to hear the tragic news over the phone, so I asked Sandy to tell you." He had also made arrangements for his parents to drive me home to West Texas. Even though the drive was only 250 miles, it was the longest ride of my life. While at first I felt nothing, reality soon hit with all the excruciating pain I could bear and more. New thoughts and realities kept creeping into my consciousness. *I'll never have grandchildren.* Or, *We've built up the land through the generations, now where will it go?* But most of all, *This just can't be! Joe's only nineteen. He's too young to die. He's my baby. NO, NO, NO!*

The next days went by in a blur. I remember little about them or about the funeral. I'm told that as I left the sanctuary of our little country church, I made a keening sound, much like a wounded animal.

Gene had been to an alcohol treatment center just prior to Joe's death but had started drinking again within a couple of weeks. However, when Joe was killed, he quit again, saying that he knew I would need him - and I did. He became my rock to lean on, though he was grieving too.

Little in my life had prepared me to deal with this tragedy. Having grown up on a small West Texas farm with an almost ideal childhood, my middle name could have been *naïve*. After graduating from the University of Texas, I thought I was ready to conquer the world, but unfortunately, the world held a few surprises for me.

I also thought I would marry the man of my dreams and live happily ever after, but that sure did not happen. The man I married, Leo, could be SO charming, then, suddenly turn on me like a rabid, vicious animal. I naively thought that with my love and devotion, he would change. Of course, he did not, and I knew that I must leave. Then, horror of horrors, I became pregnant.

I was like a little bird with broken wings in the clutches of a predator. The harder I struggled, the more abusive Leo became and the more impossible it was to leave. I had been helping him in his real estate business but knew that if I were to escape, I must have a different job. In his business, I received no money,

3

because he needed every penny for "investments."

I had been horrified to find out that I was pregnant, but Joe's birth was the best thing that ever happened to me. Leaving Leo was no longer an option - it was a must. Joe's life was now in danger. Since no shelters were available at that time, I started my job search in earnest and planned our escape. Leo had hired an attractive young woman to work in his office, so he considered my getting another job to be a good thing. I foolishly thought that I could save money to leave, but my paychecks went straight into Leo's pocket. That was part of his control. I realized that I would never have money saved, so it was now or never.

One Friday afternoon, I picked up my single week's paycheck, one-year-old Joe, and we were gone, never to return. Despite Leo's previous threats of how he would kill or maim me if I left, it did not happen. Timing was everything - Leo was now involved with another sweet young thing and my leaving was quite convenient for him.

I initially struggled with depression, but without the constant barrage of emotional abuse and fear, I climbed out of that dark hole. It took awhile. My self-esteem had been stripped from me like bark from a tree, and I had few friends. I now know that abusers isolate their victims from friends and family. The abuser must be in total control.

The following years turned out to be my happiest ever. Everyday, I picked Joe up from daycare, and the two of us would do something fun. We never did anything expensive or elaborate, but our newfound freedom was exhilarating. I usually strapped Joe into a child's seat on the back of my bike and we headed with a straggle of other kids to a nearby park where they played. We made adventures out of the simplest and silliest things, and I treasure these memories now.

When Joe was six, I met Gene, a great guy who became a loving husband to me and father to Joe. Eventually, because Gene and I both had country roots, we decided that, surely, country living would be better for all of us. We moved onto my family's old farm in West Texas, and life was good for many years. Joe grew up playing six-man football and working summers on the farm, plowing and hauling hay. He showed heifers each year, kept the heifers for breeding stock and sold the calves to help pay for college. He attended college for one year and apparently had a very good time - according to his grades. He did not pass one subject. Gene and I did not help him financially because we wanted him to realize how difficult it is to make a living without a college education. Tensions were quite high in the Cole household that summer, so he moved in with a friend in town. That was the state of things on that fateful Labor Day weekend.

I eventually found out some facts of Joe's death. He had ridden to a Labor Day party with a friend, but the friend left the party early, thinking that Joe would get another ride home. He did not. Early the next morning, at about 5:20, Joe was run over as he lay curled in a fetal position in the middle of the road on the back side of the lake. The elderly man who ran over Joe did stop, and police were called. Had he been hit earlier and left there? Had there been a fight, as an informant years later said, or had he simply started walking home and decided to lie down, thinking a friend would pick him up? Was he depressed? I will never know. He was legally intoxicated (.1) so the small county police department decided not to investigate. I should have hounded law enforcement, but I was totally destroyed and could hardly function, much less pursue legal issues.

I, like so many of you, reached out in all directions for help. Survival did not seem possible unless I received help; however, the truth was, I didn't want to survive - I wanted to be with Joe. But survive I did. I read everything I could find on grief and followed suggestions given in books, by psychologists, lecturers, and The Compassionate Friends. Finally, I went back to school and received my Masters Degree in Counseling Psychology. Because my grief journey had been so difficult, I wanted to help others if possible.

For me, it's been a long journey, and I **still** have some hard times, but for the most part, I truly love life. I appreciate every day as never before. My sincere hope is that you will find this book to be one of the stepping stones in your grief work that **helps.**

> Grief is a passion to endure. People can be stricken with it, victims of it, stuck in it. Or they can meet it, get through it, and become the quiet victors through the active, honest, and courageous process of grieving.
>
> Author Unknown

Chapter II
Physical Symptoms of Grief

Grief isn't just mental; it can also be quite physical. A myriad of *weird* symptoms may descend on us due to the extreme stress, mental anguish, and exhaustion that result from our child's death. We often feel ill or hurt in places we didn't know could hurt.

Physical symptoms appear to be as unique as our individual personalities. In surveys taken at both The Compassionate Friends and the Alive Alone National Conventions, parents reported symptoms ranging from vague aches and pains to specific maladies - fatigue and/or anxiety, terrible headaches, fast heartbeats, backaches, shortness of breath and dizziness, burning sensation in the stomach, upset stomach – the list goes on and on. Following are symptoms that many parents reported.

The Broken Heart:

Most bereaved parents understand, possibly for the first time, why so many songs, so much poetry have been written about the broken heart. We **do** feel as though our heart has been broken, as was expressed by the following **mother**:

> "Jewel recently released a song that include the words *"There's a Hole In My Heart,"* and it truly is how I feel. I never knew a heart could physically hurt all the time. I'm in great shape, and I've even seen a heart specialist. The pain is truly just a broken heart."

Actually, there is a medical basis for the pain felt in the heart when we're grieving. It is called the **broken heart syndrome,** or stress-induced cardiomyopathy. The extreme stress we feel after the death of our child causes adrenaline and other adrenaline-like chemicals in our body to skyrocket, producing symptoms like a real heart attack. Chest pain, shortness of breath, even temporary loss of consciousness may occur. This increase in stress hormones causes the small blood vessels in our heart to contract, reducing the squeezing strength of the left ventricle; consequently, less blood is pumped. Symptoms are like a real heart attack; our heart truly does hurt.

Most people recover, but unfortunately, a multitude of complications may occur - one being a real heart attack - so a doctor should be consulted. This condition is much more common in women than men.

It isn't surprising that bereaved parents have increased mortality rates. One study found that fathers have an increased mortality rate from unnatural causes while mothers have an increased mortality rate from both natural and unnatural causes.[1]*

Energy Drain:

All the simple acts involved in daily living become a chore. Some of us can't sleep, others want to sleep all the time, but either way, we accomplish little. Getting dressed, preparing the simplest of meals, being around people, holding back tears, and trying to act normal takes so much more energy than we possess. However, with time, we **will** regain our energy, and we **will** want to live again.

Memory problems:

We have trouble remembering, learning new things, and stay-

---

*Reference numbers are in the back under "End Notes" and are listed by chapter.

ing focused. Our mind is on our child and our loss. I personally felt that my brain *hurt* from all the intruding thoughts, day and night, awake or asleep. I was preoccupied with the details of Joe's death and went over them, time after time. Later, I learned that this is normal; it actually helps us accept the reality of our loss, but it is so painful. I tried everything I knew to stop doing this, to little avail. I tried the stop-smoking technique of wearing a rubber band on my wrist and snapping it every time I had an intrusive thought. Did not work. However, there was one thing that **did help**. Every time I found myself thinking about the details of Joe's death or my inadequacies as a parent, I forced myself to remember one good thing I did for or with Joe. I now wish I had written these down.

More Accident Prone?

Are we more accident prone? Probably. Our mind is often not on what we're doing. One mother wrote about having an auto accident four days after a Compassionate Friends Conference. She was not wearing a seat belt and cracked the windshield with her head.

> "I cried in the emergency room because God could've so easily taken me, and He didn't! I bargained with him on the operating table. Told Him I was ready to come home, but that if He didn't take me, I would try to live and find meaning and purpose again. So here I am at *this* year's Compassionate Friends Conference!"

These are only a few of the physical symptoms mentioned in the surveys; however, our physical symptoms **will** dissipate with time. We **will** regain our energy and feel good again. Pain-

9

ful memories slowly transcend into precious memories, and joy returns as we rediscover life and learn to appreciate the simple things in life as never before.

Chapter III
Phases of Grief For Bereaved Parents

Kubler-Ross first presented her stages of grief in 1969[C][1], and since that time, many stages or phases of grief have been presented. To me, the most accurate, flexible, and all-encompassing of these is by T. A. Rando. [2][pp. 13-22] She wrote these specifically for parental grief, but I think they pertain to all grief.

The Avoidance Phase:
I earlier mentioned how I felt nothing when first being told about Joe's death. Obviously, I was in shock, which I now consider a miracle. I do not think our bodies can physically take the mental trauma that losing a loved one causes any more than it can take a physical trauma. I also believe that vestiges of shock last considerably longer than has been acknowledged. I remember thinking of some consequences of Joe's death six months after the fact and wondering why I had not thought of them before. I now believe that remnants of shock kept me from being confronted with everything at once.

> If it weren't for the blessedness of shock, there would be no bereaved parents. Our hearts, unprotected, could not stand such mortal wounds.
>
> Martha Bittle Clark
> *"Are You Weeping With Me God"*

Closely related to shock is denial. *No, it can't be true. Somehow this is a trick. It just can't be true.* In her book, Rando contends that denial is therapeutic at this point and acts like a "buffer by allowing the parents to absorb the reality of the loss a little at a time, preventing them from being over-whelmed." [2] (pp. 3-14)

One thing that helps us face reality is viewing the body. I, for one, held out hope that the body in the casket would not be Joe's. But, it was. Evidently some parents need to see their child's body, while others do not.

> **Mother** whose son committed suicide:
> "I felt the need to go to the area where my son died and to talk to the M.E, and view pictures, as we did not have open casket. My husband was horrified at that. I couldn't accept my son's death 'til I was positive that it was him."

> **Mother** of daughter, son-in-law and granddaughter killed in fire:
> "I was not allowed to see my children after they died. It is not final for me. Probably never will be."

Eventually, our mind eases forward in increments, but as the shock and denial wane, our real pain begins.

Confrontation Stage:
Painful and sometimes volatile emotions emerge at this time, though many of these have also occurred during the shock and denial stage. Unfortunately, about the time our real pain begins, society thinks we should be over our grief by now.

The emotions associated with grief can be crippling to us

mentally if we do not work through them. Unfortunately, ignoring them does not work; they don't go away and may come out at either inopportune times or in very inappropriate ways.

> Grief is like dirty dishes....
> If you don't do them, they pile up.
> ...Author Unknown

Because the emotions in grief are so important and affect us so much, I am devoting a chapter each to Anger, Guilt, Depression, and Fear. While there are other important emotions, these seem to be major culprits that cause most of us problems. While one person may not feel guilt or one may not feel fear, we nearly all experience some of these emotions at some time or another.

Reestablishment or Accommodation Phase:
We begin to realize that we **will** survive but we will never be the same. Until now, survival almost did not seem possible or desirable, but suddenly, we just might want to **live**. We still hurt, but our grief symptoms slightly decline; we learn to live with our loss.

I have heard it said that loss of a child is like strapping a heavy load onto our back. At first, it is more than we can bear, but we slowly get used to it, and eventually, it no longer seems a burden. We know it is there, but we go about our lives and happiness can return. We focus more on our child's life, rather than dwelling on his/her death.

We do not arrive at this reestablishment phase all at once, but rather it waxes and wanes during the latter part of the confrontation phase and continues slowly thereafter. 2 (p. 22) We realize we cannot return to our past, and our future is what we make it. In my journal, two years after Joe's death, I wrote the following:

"I feel like a character in a play. Suddenly, I realize I'm in a new play and don't know my lines. I'm used to the old play. I knew my role. I was a wife, teacher, and above all, a mother. Now, here I am, in a play, living a life I know nothing about. It's very scary.

However, I think I have accepted the fact that I am in a new play, and until now, I don't believe I had. I kept hoping to somehow make my today like yesterday, rather than realizing today is a whole new day."

I have also heard parents talking about feeling their life is like a puzzle. The total picture seemed quite clear. Then, suddenly, they found themselves with new puzzle pieces that no longer fit the old picture. Basically, we have to make a new picture, using puzzle pieces from our yesterday and adding new pieces from our today. The end picture will be different, but it can still be beautiful.

Chapter IV
Anger

Is it normal to feel anger after the death of our child? You bet! We've been deprived of something very precious to us. We may direct anger towards God, doctors, ourselves, others for having complete families, and even our own beloved child for abandoning us. We become angry when people say the wrong things or avoid us, when they think we should be over it by now, or for any number of reasons. To feel anger simply means we are fighters. We are not happy with the way we feel, and by golly, we want to do something about it!

Not only is anger normal, it can be quite good. Some parents channel their anger into motivating forces to help correct injustice and/or ignorance in our society. One mother wrote about her rage towards her friends who lack sensitivity and understanding. She wrote that it still surfaces at times and is now a catalyst for her to work for the just treatment of others. Most parents whose child was murdered or whose child died because of the negligence of others are greatly motivated to seek justice, not only for their child, but for others. *Anger can be motivating or debilitating, constructive or destructive.*

We also need to remember that anger **is not** aggression. Anger is what we **feel**! Aggression is what we **do**! We can learn to deal with anger in a healthy way, rather than in a destructive way.

Ways of Dealing with Anger:

Passive Anger:
We, especially women, have often been taught from an early age that anger is wrong. We have to work to overcome this attitude. Anger is not bad; it's very normal and healthy and is actually part of the solution to our quest for healing. The problem is where we **focus** our anger. Unexpressed passive anger is usually expressed, only it often comes out as sarcasm, depression, anxiety, or a number of illnesses, such as heart disease, ulcers, asthma, or cancer.

> There is no grief like the Grief which does not speak.
> H. W. Longfellow

Passive-Aggressive Anger:
This type of anger may include forgetfulness (almost on purpose), sarcasm, procrastination, perpetual lateness, habitual fist clenching, grinding of teeth (especially at night), jaw clenching, and other exhibitions of repressed anger.

Aggressive Anger:
The limitations we need to place on ourselves when expressing anger are in the form of a simple triangle; anything is OK as long we do not harm someone else, their property or ourselves.

Do Not Harm Others...   ...Or Their Property

Do Not Harm Self

Acting Out:

A child often expresses grief by misbehaving, but adults also *act out* in self-destructive acts that unconsciously express anger or imagined guilt. Examples include driving recklessly, anesthetizing pain with chemicals, and/or *running away* by working, playing or doing anything to excess.

Mother:

"[My husband] tends to hold it in and talks little about his thoughts, using beer to drown his sorrow."

Don't attempt to drown your sorrow in drink;
You will find that sorrow can swim.

... 1890 quote

Constructive Ways to Handle Anger:

Margaret Gerner, MSW, likened our releasing anger to a tea pot. "If the steam in the pot doesn't blow off at intervals, the steam builds up and the pot blows. The stress of grief is like the boiling water in a tea pot. We need to release it periodically to prevent the damage prolonged stress does to our bodies." [1 (p. 5)]

Often we have to hurt more for a little while to hurt less eventually. To me, grief is like having a splinter in my finger. It hurts like the devil to dig it out, but then the wound can heal. Grieving is hard work, but if we try to avoid it, we will only prolong our pain and end up grieving at a later date.

Father of 17-year-old who died of cancer 15 years prior to survey:

"I stuffed my grief and buried myself in my job. I didn't work through my grief until I joined

17

The Compassionate Friends nine years later."

(Both father and mother presently work in TCF to help grieving parents cope with the catastrophic pain of their child's death.)

Tips and Techniques to Help us Deal *Constructively* with *Anger*:

Many of the following methods to deal constructively with anger are from various The Compassionate Friends newsletters, workshops and/or conventions. If you are not signed up for their newsletter, you may want to do so, because each is filled with good ideas.

Journal:

Soon after Joe's death, a good friend gave me a journal in which she wrote this message: "Betty, this little journal is for you to write down the blessings in your life." *Blessings? What blessings! She must be kidding.* I did look for blessings and found some, but I wrote much more. I will enter several of my journal entries throughout this book to hopefully let other bereaved parents know they are not crazy, they will survive, and one day they will even be happy again. For example, to show the despair I felt two years after Joe's death, I share this entry:

> "I think I truly know now what depression is. It isn't what I felt at first. I felt shock, anger, and tremendous pain, but I always had hope that I would one day be happy again. Depression is *giving up,* realizing that life will never be the same again. It will just be an endless number of pain-filled days until I die. I wouldn't admit this to others, but if I found out that I was going to die,

18

it would be such a tremendous relief. I don't think I'm going to survive."

Four years after Joe's death, I felt some happiness and actually had hope:

> "I will not say such a thing as 'I enjoy life again,' but rather that there are many things in life I enjoy. I love my garden, my yard. I have much more energy, but it comes in spurts, and my 'down and out' days are in the minority now, rather than the other way around."

However, later that year on Mother's Day, I wrote:

> "I'm darn glad I've been having good days, 'cause today's the pits, no two ways about it. When I'm down, I wonder if I'll ever be 'up' again; when I'm up, I forget how bad the 'down' days can be."

Many of the mothers and fathers in the surveys seemed to have some of their most difficult times after about two or three years following the death of their child(ren). Shock and denial no longer insulate us; we feel the raw, excruciating pain of our loss.

Mother of 18-year-old daughter killed in alcohol related car crash two years and seven months prior to survey:
"Before my daughter died, I always had hope for the future, even if things were not wonderful in the present. Now, the future looks bleak and the rest of my years will be spent in the shadow of her death."

19

Mother of 19-year-old son killed in a rock climbing accident two and one-half years before survey:

> "I seem to dwell on my son not being able to grow up, get married, have children. I want to be a grandmother, and I never will be. I feel I haven't got a future, only to grow old with my husband. I am healing. It's been 2 years and I look back and see I have progressed. It's very hard, this grief work. Sometimes it would just be easier to give up."

Those of you who are newly bereaved, do not be discouraged. Wherever you are in your grieving process is okay. Unfortunately, our friends, family, and society often think that we *should be over this by now*, right at the time of our greatest pain.

In my journal, I wrote about stressful events, and how I felt during those events. I also wrote down dreams. At the time, a dream might have had no meaning for me, but later, much later, I could reread it and understand what my subconscious was attempting to tell me. Some dreams proved to be enlightening, some painful. We apparently do much of our grief work in our sleep, which is why sleep medications should be avoided if possible.

*I wish I had written down every good, funny, happy memory of Joe as I thought of it. When a child lives, we keep making new memories, but when our child dies, we do not have that possibility. Memory fades. I now wish I could better remember the many happy times. This would also help dissipate guilt, as we could realize all the good things we did with and for our child, rather than fixate on the bad.

Besides keeping a journal, following are additional ways to work through anger and grief:

THINK about your anger so that you may recognize its true causes. Much of our anger may seem irrational to us. Unfortunately, we then not only feel angry, but we also may feel guilty for being angry. I hope I do not offend anyone, but I think my following journal entry is indicative of my initial anger towards God. Then, I felt guilty because I felt that way.

> "In Sunday School, we read, 'What you reap, you shall sow.' That's a LIE! That falls into the myth that life is fair – that the just will be rewarded, the unjust punished. Not so on this earth. Perhaps in afterlife. I hurt so-o-o-o much."

About the only time we actually reap what we sow - and then there's no guarantee - is when we are gardening or farming.

EXPRESS your anger or other emotions to a spouse, trusted friend, counselor, clergy-person, and/or support group. The value of *being heard* is immeasurable. The following old adage may certainly be true:

> If it's bad and you share it, it's half as bad.
> If it's good and you share it, it's twice as good.

Considerable research has shown that the amount and quality of social support given to a grieving parent may make more of a difference in the length and severity of grief than anything else. At first, we may have to tell our story of loss and brokenness over and over, and every time we tell our story, it becomes a little more real. Also, every time we tell our story and/or discuss our thoughts and feelings, some grief and emotions come out too.

21

> Give sorrow words; the grief that does not
> speak knits up the overwrought heart and bids it
> break.
>
> ...Shakespeare: *Macbeth*

Spouses often have a difficult time being supportive of each other because each is trying to survive his or her own intense pain. Unfortunately, family and friends may believe that since they lost the same child, their grief will be alike. Not so. Each parent had their own unique personality and relationship with the child; consequently, each will grieve a somewhat different loss. Colleen Murray, a speaker at a National TCF Convention said, "It's no wonder couples have a hard time being supportive of each other. We're like one piece of cooked spaghetti trying to hold up another." [2]

> Whomever we turn to for support needs to be
> non-judgmental and caring. A real friend is one
> who walks in when the rest of the world walks out.
> ...Walter Winchel

Support groups can be wonderful because we are with other bereaved parents who understand. Even if we are unable to express our own feelings, hearing others will help us realize how normal our crazy feelings really are. We benefit as much from listening as we do from sharing. We also receive practical advice on coping with specific problems. Many parents in the survey told of being more comfortable talking and/or listening in support groups than anywhere else.

Mother of ten-year-old daughter:
"We both attend TCF meetings regularly. He

[husband] just listens and never speaks out. He will talk one on one there after the meetings. He says he gets a lot out of the meetings by just being there. I take a more active role."

Father of 18-month-old son:
"My wife needs to talk about our child's death. I prefer to listen to other grieving parents, but I do not talk much about my feelings."

Many parents may not be comfortable with support groups. Unfortunately, I have few such opinions represented here since these surveys were taken at National support group conventions. Finding good social support may be *the find* of a lifetime.

Another way to cope with anger and/or other emotions is to **SCREAM** your rage, your anguish. A rather funny thing happened to me one day when I was inside the house, loudly screaming my rage. Since I live in the country, miles from anywhere, I thought no one was near. Unbeknownst to me, the propane man had chosen that time to re-fill my propane tank. As I was screaming out rage and anguish, I suddenly heard a timid knock on my door. I, not knowing what else to do, answered it. There stood a perplexed, red-faced man at my door, looking like he would rather be *anywhere* else but there. He hesitantly asked, "Is everything all right?"

I just calmly replied "Oh, yes. Everything's just fine." He gave me a relieved but very odd look. In fact, he still gives me odd looks!

CRY tears of sorrow, rage, whatever emotions you feel. Tears bring a release of tension and help heal a broken heart.

EXERCISE by walking, jogging, riding a bike, swimming - anything you enjoy (or once enjoyed). Physical exercises in which we have to **think** are excellent, as these not only dissipate anger and other emotions, but they also serve as a restful distraction for the mind. Examples: golf, tennis, square dancing, jazzercise, zumba, and aerobics.

POUND EMPTY EGG CARTONS WITH YOUR FIST. Or, hit a bed with a pillow or shoe; whatever works. One project I had going was cleaning antique bricks for a patio. I did not do this to release anger, stress and/or frustrations, but my hitting the mortar off those bricks with a hammer sure had that effect. Occasionally, my husband would say, "Hon, I think you need to go clean a few bricks."

GARDENING can leave us feeling exhausted but good. Besides the physical benefit of gardening, it also gives us a feeling of accomplishment, which is good for our self-esteem.

BREAK OLD DISHES YOU BUY AT GARAGE SALES. Be sure to break them some place you don't have to pick up the pieces.

DRAW OR PAINT: Art therapy is frequently used with children, but we can also benefit from its therapy. Any creative activity relieves stress.

One simple exercise is to draw an outline of your body. Where in your body do you feel pain? Using colored pencils, pens, or crayons, draw what your pain looks and feels like. Then draw captions with words to express your feelings. (EEEEEK!, ooOH! Help!)

At one point, I *threw* paint on a canvas; crimson red and *hot* orange for anger, **black** and dull grey for depression, and chartreuse yellow for my stark-raving madness. Then I ground in even more colors with a putty knife. I visualized the whole canvas being pain. When the picture dried, I ripped it and my pain, anguish, and anger to shreds. Did it help? I don't know. I think the many things I tried all worked together to help.

24

Any hobby that you enjoyed before will likely give you some relief now. Try new hobbies. I now love to quilt and I love to dance.

RELAXATION techniques that symbolically seek out the pain in your body and cause it to leave may help. Can't hurt. I listened to relaxation tapes when trying to sleep. They kept the demons of *thought* away – all those intrusive thoughts of Joe's death and my *should haves*.

We are hurting *no one*, or *anyone's property*, or *ourselves* by doing these things; we are only releasing tension, which is good and healthy.

Chapter V
Guilt

Guilt has been my Achilles heel throughout my grief journey. I could handle other emotions, but guilt crept into my mind and attached itself with deep tentacles. Thoughts of what I *should have* or *should not have* done were relentless, sparing no mercy on my beleaguered mind. It mattered not where I was or what I was doing, guilt found me. Even though I have worked hard on this emotion, I still have to battle it at times. In this chapter, I have shared many ideas and techniques that have helped me.

First, we may have to challenge previously held beliefs that likely are not true, like the **Myth of Perfect Parenthood**, first discussed by Margaret Gerner.[1]

> "The feeling of worthlessness is strong in many bereaved parents...We expect that we will raise perfect children, provide them with the very best we can afford, and most of all, see that they are safe and secure in their lives. Then when the unspeakable happens and our child dies, we feel we failed totally and completely." [1]

Even though we may *know* it isn't true, we feel that if we had been doing our job of parenting correctly, our child would be alive. As one mother stated, "I should have known something was wrong with my son, for mothers are supposed to know their children. So I feel guilty."

We may have had a very loving relationship with our child, yet we tend to fixate on the negative times or things that happened, and we probably all had times when we had a not-so-loving relationship with our child. We said things we wish we had not said, or we failed to handle situations correctly. Perhaps we failed to stop our child from doing something that we *now* realize had disastrous results, so we *now* realize we could have handled situations differently. However, if we were put in the same situation again and knew only what we knew then, we likely would make the same decisions.

Guilt comes in all types and sizes, but nearly all types play havoc with our emotions. Reading about the different types of guilt and understanding the normality of our feelings may help us work through these painful self-inflicted emotions. Margaret Miles and Alice Demi, in Therese Rando's book, *Parental Loss of a Child ©*, list six types of guilt: Parental Role, Death Causation, Survivor, Grief (grieving "too long"), Moral, and Illness Related Guilt. [2]

Parental Role Guilt:

When we are growing up, we perceive ourselves as someday becoming the perfect wife and mother, or husband and father. Even adult children plan to someday be more loving and spend more time with their parents. Then, when a loved one dies, this dream is eternally taken from us. We feel guilty for unfulfilled plans, but we need to remember that we are not perfect. Nor was our loved one. So, let's have a little forgiveness in our heart for ourselves.

How can we relieve this guilt? Psychologist and Grief Workshop Facilitators often have us write a letter to our child, telling him or her all the things we wish we had done differently. Ask for his/her forgiveness. Then, read the letter aloud in front of his/her favorite chair or to their picture. We may feel ridiculous doing this, but I believe it does bring some healing.

Then, you can take it one step further and reverse the dialogue. Sit in your child's chair and tell yourself what you actually believe your son or daughter would say to you. When I did this, I was surprised by what "Joe" said. You may want to keep the letter you wrote to your child or burn it, symbolically releasing the guilt.

While getting my Masters Degree, I practiced this skill at a "Healing the Wounded Heart Conference," a conference given to help us uncover and refute irrational ideas.[3] I knew that the all-consuming guilt I felt after Joe's death HAD to be somewhat irrational, and I tried nearly everything in an attempt to get rid of it.

In this conference, we were given several exercises, then were told to write a letter <u>from</u> our lost love. In my case, Joe would tell me *his* feelings and *his* responsibility in what happened. (This would not be applicable in all cases.) What would he say? For some reason, this helped relieve some of my guilt. Following is my letter from Joe.

> Dear Mama,
>
> I love you. I was selfish in thinking only about me. Please forgive me for denying you so many things...being with me, knowing the wife I would have selected, grandchildren, being there for you to hug, popping in to say hello and talking about what's going on in our lives.
>
> Please forgive my self-destructive behavior and for not considering you, Sara, Dad, my friends. I'm sorry my actions and absence have caused you so much pain. When I destroyed my life, or my life was destroyed, I almost destroyed

your life too.

I love you and forgive you.

Love,

Joe

We use a form of irrational self-talk when we make self-statements that use words like *should, ought, always* and *never*. My words were definitely *should have*. Even though I knew that many of my *should haves* were irrational, I could not seem to internalize this fact. In the workshop, we were told that if we are beating ourselves up because we think we failed to live up to certain standards, we need to examine the standards. Are the standards themselves realistic? Are we beating ourselves up for things that we have done many times before and other parents also do routinely without ill effects?

But, I also had to realize that some of my guilt was **real**, and there was simply nothing I could do but forgive myself. One Mother told me something that helped: "Any mistakes I made, I made out of ignorance–because I always had my child's best interest at heart." None of us chose for our child to die. We may feel somehow responsible, but if we had our choice, our child would be alive.

Guilt is an emotion that seems to wash over us again and again. We think we have put something behind us, then it rears its ugly head again, and we have to work through it one more time. Be patient with yourself. Set small goals. For real guilt, forgive yourself. Turn guilt into regret.

Death Causation Guilt:

We place unrealistic expectations on ourselves regarding the preventability of death. No matter what the cause of death, we often believe that at some point, we could have prevented it. We *should have* made them go to the doctor, or recognized their depression, or taken them to school, rather than permitting them to ride their bike. However, with some decisions, like making someone go to the doctor or preventing a suicide, we had little, if any, choice. For other decisions, we did what we thought best at the time. How could we have known that, on that particular day, we should have done something differently to protect our child?

Survivor Guilt:

We never dreamed we would outlive our child. That just is not the way the world is supposed to work, so, when our child dies, we feel guilty. *It should have been me. I'm the next in line.*

Survivor guilt is also common in those coming back from war. They may wonder why he or she survived and *those more deserving to live*, did not.

Grief Guilt:

Grief usually lasts longer and is more intense than we ever realized possible; consequently, we may feel guilty because we're not *over it yet*. About a year after Joe's death, an uncle told me, "You just have to get over it and move on," *as if I had a choice.* I wondered if he would say that if I had a migraine or if one of my legs had been ripped off. I certainly felt a part of me had been savagely torn away. Unfortunately, besides feeling hurt and anger when he said that, I also thought "maybe I *should* be doing better." The attempts by others to help can actually hurt. Our mental wounds can be just as crippling as physical wounds, but they get so little respect!

> Every one can master a grief but he that has it.
> …Shakespeare:
> *Much Ado About Nothing*

We may feel guilty because we over-reacted at the time of death, or seemingly felt nothing. We may have lashed out at other family members or isolated ourselves. Because of our intense grief, we may fail to be supportive of others in the family, or we feel that we're a poor mother to our other children, or wife or husband to our mate. Again, we need to be patient with ourselves.

Moral Guilt:

Why me, Lord? What did I do to deserve this? We search for answers. The world is no longer a safe and orderly place where good things happen to good people. Our belief system has been attacked. If we previously believed, *We get what we deserve,* or *What goes 'round comes 'round,* then we have to mesh together previously held beliefs with what we now know as real: *bad things do happen to good people.*

Many of us struggle with moral guilt. Some researchers believe that our moral guilt may stem from early religious teachings. Dr. John Claypool, Episcopalian minister and author of several grief related books, said the following:

> "Whenever religion has injected a note of judgment and condemnation into the grieving experience, it has not only stepped beyond the bounds to which any human being has a right to step, but it also puts guilt into the mix of grief, and therefore just adds to the burden. This kind of religious emphasis may be a part of the problem, rather than being part of the answer." [4]

The one thing that helped me more than any other with moral guilt was Rabbi Harold Kushner's book, *When Bad Things Happen to Good People ©.* His son, Aaron, died of progeria, the rapid aging disease. In the book, he argues that bad things happen randomly regardless of our personal deservingness. "Life is not fair; the wrong people get sick and the wrong people get robbed and the wrong people get killed in wars and accidents." He further states that attempting to justify a tragedy by speaking of God's will, may only complicate the tragedy. [5 (142)] However, I do realize that just because this book helped me, it may not help you. What helps one may not help another.

Illness Related Guilt:

When our loved one dies after a lengthy illness, we may rake ourselves over the coals for things we wish we had done differently. Caregivers often become so physically and emotionally exhausted that the simple act of staying awake can become a major challenge. Yet, we expect ourselves to remain cheerful, have infinite patience and energy, and always be there for our loved one; but we are human. No matter how much we love someone, there will be times when we feel anger or resentment towards them. When our own body and mind scream for rest, it is natural to become irritable. Then, when our loved one dies, we feel guilty for all the things we wish we had said or done differently.

We possibly secretly or openly wished for their death, longing to end their suffering and our own. However, when death does come, our initial reaction may be relief, soon to be followed by guilt for feeling relief. We wonder how we could have ever wished for their death, but we need to think back, truly remember their pain and suffering, and when we do, we will likely realize we would not want them back to endure more pain.

Sometimes we feel guilt because we were or were not there at the time of death, or we did or did not enact measures to prolong their life. We made the best choices we could with the information we had at the time. Think back to the choices you had and why you made the decisions you did. Tell yourself, "I did the best I could with what I knew at the time."

One last idea to help relieve our guilt: From Richard Paul Evans, *The Four Doors* ©.

We often try and condemn ourselves over and over for something we should or should not have said or done. Even though we do not allow **double jeopardy** in our court systems, we often *try* and *punish* ourselves over and over for some real or imagined "crime".

What can we do? The next time we berate our self for some guilt for which we've already suffered, call it out. Identify exactly what happened, when, and how many times we've already punished ourself for that same mistake. (Approximate) Remember, we all make mistakes!

Then say to yourself, "I know that I did wrong, but I've already paid for my mistake. Punishing myself over and over for what I've already suffered is unjust to me and God. I hereby finally forgive myself and let it go forever." Even though our guilty "crimes" will likely rear their ugly heads again, if we continue to *call them out* and refute them, they will weaken and may totally go away. [6 (pp. 76-79)] *

* Reprinted with the permission of Simon & Schuster, Inc. from THE FOUR DOORS: A Guide to Joy, Freedom, and a Meaningful Life by Richard Paul Evans. Copyright © 2013 by Richard Paul Evans. All rights reserved.

Chapter VI
Depression, the Insidious Invader

Depression creeps into our mind, body and spirit like a noxious dark fog, slowly enveloping us and leaving us almost powerless in its wake. I felt like a body snatcher had crept upon me, invading parts of my mind and body, leaving me with a myriad of horrid symptoms. It is theorized that our brain does literally tire from being continually bombarded by stimuli, making it less able to perform normal brain functions. This would account for disturbances in memory and attention, muscular functions and in sleep, as well as various other manifestations.

I know nothing of poetry, but somehow, even an attempt at poetry helps us express pain and sorrow. I could find no poem that expressed the horrible darkness of depression, yet ended with hope, so I wrote the following:

The depressive yoke of despair renders me powerless.
I cry out in pain and frustration.
Where has the happiness of my yesterday gone?

Barnacled branches of guilt pierce and stab my soul,
Showing no mercy.
Oh, God. Where has my yesterday gone?

I can't bear the pain. The terrible pain.
Will I never again know

34

Joy, or peace or happiness? My yesterday **is** gone.

But then, from the bottomless pit of despair...
I look up. Surely not!
There! Is that a glimpse of sunshine?

Amazingly, from the depths and shards of grief,
A miraculous ray of hope appears,
Lighting the way to joy and
happiness for a new tomorrow.
......Charlene Cole

Immediately after our child's death, we seem to have more hope of being happy again *someday* than we do two or three years down the road. At this point, shock and denial are gone and reality sets in. We wonder, *Will I ever again know happiness, or has it forsaken me forever?* We are very susceptible to depression at this time.

Symptoms of Major Depression:

What are the symptoms of depression? Just as grief is as individual as a fingerprint, so is depression. However, we do experience similarities in symptoms.

To "qualify" for major depression, we must have experienced five of the following symptoms within a continuous two-week period. Also, either symptom number one and/or number two must be included in this five. I have no doubt that all bereaved parents meet the criteria for major depression at some time during our grief journey. Just two weeks? Two months? Two years?

1. Depressed mood most of the day, nearly every day.

In depression, a dark shadow seems to hang over our world, removing the color and vibrancy from everything we see and touch. Everything is a reminder of what we've lost.

How can we not be in a depressed mood after our child's death? Not only is our precious child gone from our life, but our world as we knew it has collapsed. Old friends may fade away at a time we need them most. Our whole value system has likely been thrown into the air and fallen shattered at our feet. We have to slowly pick up the pieces and re-evaluate what we now believe. Priorities have changed. We now better understand the randomness of tragedies. At a time when our pain is so deep that it threatens our very being, we're having to restructure our whole belief system. So, **yes**, we likely are depressed.

Symptoms of serious **grief** and **depression** are nearly the same. I struggled with depression and/or grief symptoms, but with time, their severity grew less and their duration shorter. After a few years, periods of depression usually occurred around important dates or when something else was going on in my life.

I have learned to *make plans* for times I know *might* be difficult – plan a trip, immerse myself in some planned activity, or surround myself with happy people that will be okay if I suddenly start crying. Of course, we don't always see "down times" coming; sometimes they sneak upon us like a thief in the night and waylay our best intentions.

A few years after Joe's death, I found myself in a depressive episode where I was always on the brink of tears. Hopelessness and despair enveloped me, and I couldn't shake it. One day, my sister-in-law said, "Betty, you look like you are constantly about to cry. Are you all right?" Of course, I broke down at that time. She had unknowingly given me permission to cry out my misery. At any rate, she and my brother had a trip to New York City planned and asked me to go with them. The different atmosphere and location were wonderful respites for my grief. I seemed to turn a corner and finally shake that time of depression. After that, I continued to have periods of depression, but every year, they grew less severe and easier to conquer.

Actually, depression is a part of our healing, though we sure do not like it. Through grief and depression, we will hopefully separate from our previously held hopes and dreams and move on to new realities with new hopes and dreams.

2. Loss of interest or pleasure in all or nearly all activities most of the day, nearly every day.

Even though I had always enjoyed being around people, I just wanted to stay home. When I did go out, I could think of nothing to say – my mind was on Joe. Were people talking about me? Were my parenting skills being questioned? I probably stood around like a wallflower attempting to smile but looking like I had just eaten a persimmon. I didn't fit in. As soon as possible, I would find some excuse to leave; however, once home, I would still be miserable.

Mother:
> "I used to play bridge. Now, can't concentrate.
> Used to enjoy tennis. Now, no energy. Just want to
> flop down on the sofa, watch movies and forget."

Activities that require exercise **and** thought seemed to work best for me. However, *making myself* do any activity was another matter. I found anything creative to be helpful, whether it be painting, drawing, sewing, making collages, writing or any other creative endeavor. Men (and women) often find relief when working with wood or metal.

3. Sleep Disturbances:

We may want to sleep all the time or we wake up in the middle of the night and can't go back to sleep.*

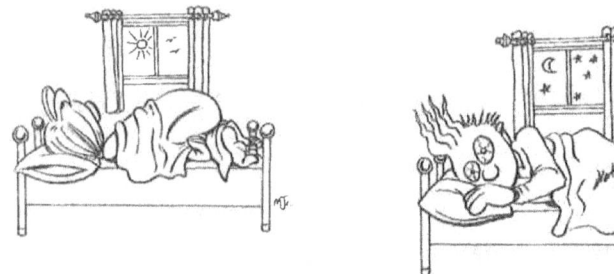

Lying in bed I wonder, "When will it be day?"
Risen I think, "How slowly evening comes!"
Restlessly I fret till twilight falls.

Job 7:4

Many parents wrote of sleep problems. I personally felt exhausted, yet could not sleep. If I awakened anytime after 2:00 AM, I allowed myself to get up; otherwise, I would lie there thinking of all the horrible details of Joe's death or go through the *if onlys* and *should haves* the rest of the night.

Because we do much of our grief work in our sleep, it is advised that we do not take sleep medications if possible. Sometimes we become so mentally and physically exhausted, we have to occasionally take something to help us get a good nights' sleep.

---

* All drawings in this chapter are by Michael Jones, Director of Art, Hardin-Simmons University, Abilene, Texas.

Dreams can be very revealing. Keep a pad by your bed to record your dreams – if you can remember them. My dreams often seemed to have no meaning, but months or years later, I would understand what they were trying to tell me. Some dreams helped, some hurt, but they often revealed something I had not realized or confronted before.

Dream from my journal:

"I was listening to a lecture when the speaker said that my son Joe's death was drug-related. *Why did he say that? And in front of all these people that I don't know.* Then he repeated his statement. *Not true! How could he say that?*"

Later I realized it was true. Joe had been to a party, alcohol was in his blood, and most likely, he would not have been run over had he not been drinking. I had been discounting this fact – giving myself more credit (and guilt) for his death than I likely deserved. Also, it portrayed how concerned I was with the opinion of others.

4. **Low self-esteem. Feelings of worthlessness or excessive or inappropriate guilt.**

The **Myth of Perfect Parenthood** (discussed in chapter V) is one factor that leads to our having poor self-esteem. We may think, *If I couldn't save my child, what good am I?* All of our previous successes seem so minor, our failures so significant. Even though we may *know* that our guilty feelings are somewhat irrational, we tend to torture ourselves with *should haves* and *if onlys*. The negative things we did when our child was alive seemed so insignificant at the time, but after our child's death, they become monstrous demons. Tsunamis of guilt wash over us.

A good friend or family member can be invaluable in disputing our negative thinking. When we become obsessed with all the things we did wrong, they can dispute these with things we did right. "Oh, don't you remember when you... That was such an act of love." TELL your friends how they can help you. Educate them.

If we're dependent on ourselves to dispute our own negative thinking, we may have to FORCE ourselves to look for the positive things we did with and for our child. Write them down. These good memories will be precious to you later. (Read the chapter on "Guilt" for ideas.)

5. **Stuff or Starve! Significant weight gain or weight loss when not dieting.**

What is considered a significant weight loss or gain? A change of 5% of your body weight in a month is considered to be significant.

Mother:
> "He drank and smoked. I stuffed my face."

6. **Feeling tired OR half wired.**

Physical exhaustion may keep us from accomplishing anything but the smallest tasks...if we can remember what they were! On the flip side, some parents experience anxiety and jump from task to task, still accomplishing little. Unfortunately, we may experience these symptoms intermittently. Following are examples of each:

Mother of a 33-year-old daughter who died of natural causes - 19 months since death:
> "I stayed strong at the beginning, while my

husband became increasingly depressed and unable to function. He had suicidal thoughts but improved after going into therapy...He continues with both. I had a great need to stay busy at first but now cannot summon the energy to do more than the basics required to function."

Mother of 21-year-old son who died from bone marrow transplant complications - less than four months since death:

"I watch a lot of TV to distract me. My husband spends most of his free time working on our house, while I find I have very little energy and must force myself toward activity."

Mother of a 25-year-old son who died in an accident - about four years since death:

"I do suffer anxiety, wondering what is next, although my worries now are broad, whereas before, I had specific things that worried me. I really don't feel I have any control over things."

7. Irritability. Distraught by things that normally would not bother you.

Mother:

"Five or six months after my son's death, I started seeing a psychologist because I was so angry all the time - sometimes bordering on rage. I never considered hurting myself or anybody else, I just snapped people's heads off and flew into a ranting fit - because the ice cream was gone when I wanted it. She (the psychologist) released me after three or four months, and after nineteen months, I am better."

8. Have difficulty concentrating, making decisions, finishing tasks.

Do you stand in the middle of a room, wondering what you're there to get? Forget in the middle of a sentence what you were going to say? Do people ask you the stupidest questions? My cousin had the nerve to ask why I had hot pads in the fridge. Doesn't everyone? (I'm sure you can give me some *really good* examples.)

Father:

"My wife has suffered from depression and is going to professional counseling. Things such as forgetfulness and inability to make decisions continue to be a real problem."

Mother:

"He (husband) was able to read and concentrate. I wasn't able to do either. He stopped sleeping. I slept more. I had bouts of anxiety, he didn't."

9. Suicidal thoughts.

It is not that we really want to die, we just want to be with our child and free of pain.

This was expressed by both mothers and fathers in the survey. In response to the question, "Have you and your husband grieved differently?" one mother wrote: "He wants to die. I want to live for my son. He does not believe in eternal life. I do. He has no hope. I do." Another mother wrote: "No fear of death. I consider suicide. I wonder what purpose I have in life. He was an only child.

Some in the survey didn't express suicidal thoughts as such, but they wanted the pain to end.

Mother, two years since death:_

"[My] hopes and dreams are gone, even with surviving children. Life often seems empty and meaningless, and I want it to finish, end."

Mother, 16 months since death:

"Life doesn't mean much anymore. I cannot see why I'm still here. I wish the end would be soon so the pain would disappear. I hate having to be here, resent seeing others not appreciating their children. Life sucks."

Thoughts of wanting our life to end dissipate with time. Apparently, very few bereaved parents actually take their own lives. One way to feel better about ourselves is to help others.

Other signs of depression:
1. Feelings of aloneness and isolation.

We feel different, like we don't belong. One *mother* expressed the way many of us feel: "[I] felt like a neon sign flashing 'Dead Child' beamed from my head." So much of society, sometimes even our friends and family expect us to *put on a happy face* and *get on with our lives*.

43

Mother, two years since death of daughter)

"My kids actually tried to do an *intervention* on me. They thought I should be over my grief by now, or at least doing better! I said 'Wait one minute here!', but I didn't convince them. Here I am at a TCF convention and realize *I'm quite normal!"*

We may feel totally abandoned by some and get lectured by others.

> The real art of conversation isn't only to say
> The right thing at the right time,
> But to leave unsaid the wrong thing
> At the tempting moment.
> ...Author Unknown

Oh, but what we would love to say.

Another reason we may isolate ourselves is to "lick our wounds". Research has shown that pre-occupation with the details of our child's death is one of the ways we actually recover and rebuild our lives.

2. Lack of sex drive or desire more sex.

The following entries were by **mothers:**

Nine months since child's death:

"My husband is able to think about being sexually active, whereas I want nothing to do with sex."

44

15 months since child's death:

"I wanted sex to reaffirm our love. My husband's response was "How can you think of sex at a time like this?" It was unthinkable for him. I was able to understand his point of view and respect it. He, in return, was able to hold and cuddle me so I felt loved."

Six years since death:

"Our affection for each other has gotten stronger. Our sex life has been non-existent at times. He is not understanding about my loss of libido."

It is important to the healing process that we face and work through the pain and heartaches. We can't get *over* or *around* our grief without working *through* it. If we deny or run from our feelings, those feelings and emotions will be waiting for us when we quit running. We simply have to hurt for awhile.

Depression, like all grief emotions, does recur from time to time. We learn to plan ahead for times we know will be difficult. However, sometimes, it just sneaks up on us. We all have our ups and downs.

Problems To Avoid:

Attempts to block feelings:

Drugs and/or Alcohol:

Self medicating may dull the grief symptoms, but it also prolongs the grief process and may create even more problems. One *mother* stated: "One of us became an alcoholic. The other, co-dependent. We are both being counseled for our problems."

Over activity, Work:

It is not uncommon for one or the other bereaved parent to work to excess, as expressed by one *mother*: "My spouse worked endlessly. Seven years after the death of our daughters, we formed a TCF Chapter. Then, he did his grief work."

Try to find geographic cure by traveling or moving:

It is recommended that we make no major changes within one year of our child's death--no divorces, no drastic moves or decisions.

Mother:

"My husband wanted to immediately dispose of our daughter's belongings, sell our house and move six hundred miles away to new surroundings. I was more inclined to hold on to everything and 'stay put.' I could not bear the thought of selling the house where she grew up, getting rid of all her belongings and moving to an area where I knew no one."

When To Seek Help For Depression:

1. If you have a PLAN with your suicidal thoughts. Most of us

feel that we want to be with our child and end the pain, but if you are seriously thinking of taking your own life, do seek GOOD professional help, preferably someone with considerable knowledge about depression and grief. Medication may be given, not as a means of coping with grief, but as a way of getting through a period of intense feeling until we're better able to cope with our tremendous pain. Anti-depressants take some time to *kick in,* and may not work once they do.

2. If you have a previous history of depression or any form of mental illness, you may have a predisposition to severe problems again. I had experienced a significant depression after my first marriage and may have been more susceptible to depression. However, I do not believe that I experienced much more depression than other bereaved parents. That is another benefit of bereaved parent support groups; they are a good barometer for how we are doing in our own grief work.

3. If you remain depressed too long. How long is too long? I have read everywhere from two weeks to fourteen months. However, I would say, it never hurts to seek professional help at **any** time. Just get a **good** professional familiar with grief!

4. If you develop symptoms of the illness from which your child suffered.

Suggestions For Ways To Take Care Of Yourself:
The same suggestions given for working through anger and guilt apply here too. Guilt plays a significant role in depression. Don't forget to take care of yourself.

1. Take care of your body.
   Eat right.
   Exercise.

Get plenty of rest.

2. Avoid stressful situations. Learn to say "No." Often, bereaved parents do become more assertive and say "NO" when asked to do things because we realize we HAVE to take care of ourselves if we want to survive.

3. Be very patient and kind to yourself. Do things that feel good to you, whether it be a luxurious bubble bath, a massage, or whatever.

4. Spend time every day doing something you enjoy.

5. Make your goals short term. Give yourself stars, mental or otherwise, when you accomplish something. I have a friend who always makes a *to-do list* of things she plans to accomplish the next day. After the death of her child, she still made the lists, but the many things that did not get done were replaced with things she *did* do. She shared some of her *accomplishments*.

   1. Got out of bed and was kinda' pleasant to my husband.
   2. Made wonderful peanut butter sandwiches for lunch.
   3. Went to grocery store and didn't have to be physically removed for crying all over the Cocoa Puffs.

   She felt better and we had a good laugh.

6. Have a *Spirit Lifter Box*. Whenever someone says something good about you or compliments you, write it down. Read these when times get tough. Years before Joe's death, I had attended a meeting where everyone wrote something nice or something we admired about every other person in the room. Then, we handed them out. I brought mine home, somewhat

48

shocked at the good things my friends had said about me and put them into a plastic disposable "Better-Than-Butter" container to stash in a bottom drawer. Years after Joe's death, I ran across these, read them, and they helped me feel better about myself. In fact, I found such satisfaction from reading these scraps of paper that I transferred them into a pretty crystal dish. I occasionally pulled one or more out to read, and they lifted my spirits.

7. Educate the public. Bereaved parents often feel a need to speak to students, teachers and other groups about various self-destructive activities, usually pertaining to whatever killed their child. Examples include recognizing signs of possible suicidal behavior and helping with suicide prevention. One mother gives speeches to help educate people about AIDS to help them better understand the disease. One couple designs and sells donor organ T-shirts to raise awareness of the need, and proceeds go to the hospital where their child was waiting for a heart transplant.

Several mothers and fathers were affiliated with MADD. Many parents spoke to various groups about grief and how to be supportive to a grieving person. Several in the survey, I for one, should have talked with police departments about recognizing and being sensitive to grief. There are so many ways we can educate. If nothing else, we can educate our friends and family.

8. Create memorials, give scholarships or time in memory of your child. This helps us feel that our child's life was not in vain and that he or she is continuing to live on in some way. We feel good when we accomplish something positive in our child's name.

From the survey, I found that many parents have totally

changed their lives since the death of their child(ren). Some furthered their education to help in fields they believed to be beneficial and helpful to others. Some wrote books to educate and/or to help other grieving individuals. Many gave very simple gifts; some gave quite expensive endowments and trusts. Others gave of their time to help others and/or to make the earth a more beautiful place to live.

Chapter VII
Fear And Anxiety

Fear? Why would I feel fear? The worst thing that can happen **has** **already** *happened;* but I was in for a rude awakening. Fears descended on me that I had never known before. After reading the surveys, I realized that many of us experience fear of one kind or another at some point in our grief journey.

1. The number-one fear expressed by parents was *fear for remaining children and other family members*:

Father of 22-month-old daughter:

"[I now have a] constant awareness of my wife's and my surviving son's mortality. I think about the loss of one of them almost constantly."

Mother of 14-year-old daughter:

"I fear for the safety of my other children... I wonder if I am a good mother.

If I could not protect one of my kids, how can I protect the others?"

2. We may *fear our own death* because we suddenly realize that today may be the last day for ourselves or someone we love.

Mother of seven-year-old and three-year-old
killed in accident 11 months before survey:

"I find that at this stage I fear death, and I do not understand why. I would think I would not want to live, and I sometimes don't. I am very confused."

Parents of homicide victims suddenly feel that the world is

not a safe place. The basic trust they had in other individuals is shattered; thus they often experience fear for themselves and their remaining family members, especially if the perpetrator of the crime is still at large.

3. We *fear an unknown future.* It is comforting to believe we control our own destinies, so we often deceive ourselves into believing we have more control than we really do. Then, when the unthinkable happens and our child dies, we realize that we have so much less control than we thought, and it is a scary new world.

Mother of 19-year-old that died from Leukemia and A.M.L.:

"Through my son's death, I have seen that no matter how hard you fight, or how hopeful you feel, there is no real control over the timing of our child's death."

The belief that we have more control than we actually do starts when we're babies. Everything at that time revolves around our wants and needs. If we're hungry, we cry, and we get fed. Or perhaps someone makes *goo-goo* eyes at us, we smile, and our parents get so excited. We caused it. We controlled our world. This sounds silly, but it's true.

We can read about child development and grief theories all day, but there is nothing like personal experience to bring it home. My step-granddaughter, Ambra, about four years old, was staying with us, and we were heading to church. I was desperately trying to get her to hurry. "Ambra, we're going to be late if we don't hurry." Sure enough, we arrived at the church late, and we could hear the organ already playing. I said, "Oh, Ambra. I guess they've already started. I hear the music."

About that time, the song ended, and Ambra said, "I don't

hear it, Mimi."

"Well, they've stopped now."

"OH! Is that because they know we're coming?"

We grow out of this *self-centeredness* to a great extent but keep some of it. As adults, we still like to think we have more control than we do. If we go to the races and we win, we may believe our *red cap* made us lucky, so we wear it the next day, hoping to win again. And, *us Sutherners* eat black-eyed peas on New Year's Day for good luck. We know better....but just in case! Then, when the unbelievable happens and our child dies, we realize we do not have as much control as we thought. We have to weave together what we previously believed and what we now know as reality.

Why do friends and acquaintances sometimes say the *exact wrong thing*? There is a tendency to believe that the world is a just and fair place, and victims of misfortune must have done something to deserve their fate. "You get what you deserve and deserve what you get." This *just world assumption* is an *adaptive illusion* that enables people to believe that their own good fortune is deserved, rather than being random luck. They are good parents, so such misfortune could not happen to them.

When someone hears of a child's death, they often ask, "Was he drinking?" Or they rationalize, "Well, he always was wild." In their mind, they're trying to find a reason it happened to your child instead of their own. Thankfully, many of our true friends are still there for us, realizing that "There, but for the grace of God, go I..."

Anxiety attacks sometimes occur with bereaved individuals, especially after sudden, violent deaths.

After my husband's death (story in *Suicide Chapter*), I felt very anxious, like I could jump out of my skin. The first time I went to Dallas to see friends, I approached one of the multi-level bridge interchanges and felt a little apprehension, which wasn't unusual because I do not like heights. However, as I started up the bridge, I panicked. I began hyper-ventilating, my heart started thundering in my chest and ears, and I broke out in a cold sweat. I felt I simply could not go over that bridge and live. I hate to admit this now, but I backed down that bridge. Thankfully, no cars were coming. I also knew that by giving in to this phobia, I was strengthening it.

However, I started working on this problem, though not right away. At first, a friend rode with me over the lower bridges, casually talking all the while. For some reason, the slight distraction of her carrying on a normal conversation helped tremendously. Also, I knew that she could take over if I totally lost control. Later, I would cross the bridge on my own - with fear - but I did it. Every trip to Dallas, I would either work on my *last feat*, or repeat the process with a little higher bridge. I spent much time lost on back roads because I could not go the short way – across a bridge.

I eventually conquered my phobia, but I have new respect for those who suffer with anxiety of any type. While my phobia seemed to be a somewhat temporary problem, some people suffer greatly with anxiety.

Following is the story of one of my former student's severe anxiety following her husband's suicide:

Amy's Story:

"I had suffered anxiety attacks in the past; however, with medication, I thought they were under control. Even though I had been under tremendous stress due to Alvin's increasing drug addiction, I had not experienced an attack for six months. However, after Alvin's suicide, I experienced terrible flashbacks. I would be driving

Alvin   Alvin, Amy, Tori & James

along, and suddenly, the horrific image of Alvin, purple faced, tongue protruding as he hung from the bungee cord, would appear. Immediately, I would go into a full blown anxiety attack.

I went to the hospital three times, each time really believing I was having a heart attack. My blood pressure and pulse would be off the charts, but I was having anxiety attacks, not heart attacks. Due to my fear of having an attack, I didn't drive, and for two years, I rarely left home. I bought books, checked the internet, talked with others, including therapists, and my attacks are once again under control.

I called my 'blood family' (I'm adopted), and learned that most of my immediate family is on anxiety medication. There must be a genetic tendency for anxiety attacks. The doctor has worked with me to find a medication that really works **for me**. What works for one may not work for another."

Post Traumatic Stress Disorder:

Besides anxiety, Amy was likely experiencing symptoms of Post Traumatic Stress Disorder, which is not unusual, especially in traumatic deaths. Symptoms of PTSD may include intrusive thoughts pertaining to the death or last conversations, poor concentration, sleep disorders, nightmares, depression, fear, extreme anger, feelings of detachment or being different than others, and other symptoms. Sounds like us, doesn't it? Actually, most of us do experience some symptoms of PTSD, especially if the death was sudden.

Even though I did not see Joe's death, scenes from his death played repeatedly in my mind. The *movie*, with all its horrid details, played over and over, giving me little relief. All of my life, I had struggled to remember names, places, and events; now, I just wanted to forget. My mind resembled a kaleidoscope, slowly turning without my bidding. The tasks I tried to perform would be forgotten, as unbidden thoughts of Joe's death or of my inadequacies as a parent intruded. I wandered from room to room, wondering what I was there to do. Eventually, the unwanted thoughts dissipated, disappearing entirely for longer and longer periods of time. Now, I think of Joe's **life**, not his death – usually – but there are still moments. I believe our mind's ability to forget is a wonderful thing. I never thought I would say that.

If you are having severe symptoms, you need to take measures to help yourself. Reading about symptoms and possible solutions, either in books or on the Internet, may help. Amy mentioned that when she feels an attack coming on, she calls a friend if possible. Just having a normal conversation can be therapeutic. Support groups are often beneficial because we learn tips and techniques for handling our fears and anxiety, and it *always* helps to know we are not alone. If your symptoms are severe, therapists now have wonderful methods to lessen anxiety. Time helps, but time alone usually does not heal. We must work with time.

ANY trauma, like war, natural disasters, rape, incest and child abuse, traumatic accidents or deaths may cause PTSD. Whatever causes this syndrome in individuals is usually experienced with intense horror and helplessness. **We** certainly felt horror and helplessness, didn't we?

The prevalence of PTSD following the violent death of a child has been found to be twice as high for men and three times as high for women than for those in the general population, even five years after the death. However, for most of us, we work through these symptoms, just like we work through the other symptoms of grief.

Our fears may overwhelm us at first, but if we meet them face to face, we eventually become the victor and become stronger than we have ever been before.

> You gain strength, courage, and confidence by every experience in which you really stop to look fear in the face. You are able to say to yourself, "I lived through this horror, I can take the next thing that comes along."
>
> Eleanor Roosevelt

Or we can be a little more rowdy with this barroom song:

> OH, the liquor was spilt on the bar room floor
> And the bar was closed for the night,
> When the little gray mouse came out of his hole

And sat in the pale moon light.
He lapped up the liquor off the bar room floor,
As on his haunches he sat.
And all night long you could hear him roar...
BRING ON THAT DANG OLE CAT!
Contributed by my friend, Debbie Maines

Chapter VIII
Grief Characteristics
Common To Bereaved Parents

Nearly all bereaved parents experience *some* similar emotions and issues, regardless of the age of their child or how they died. Following are characteristics of our special grief that are not mentioned elsewhere in this book.

1. Every member of a family has roles, other than just *mother* or *father*. The father may have loved playing catch with his son on weekends, or cherished the times his daughter ran to greet him when he returned from work. Since these roles cannot be replaced, we sometimes have to change our routines to lessen our pain. When our child is taken from us suddenly, the roles they played in our lives are also taken from us suddenly, throwing us into further limbo.

   I heard one facilitator compare a family to a warm chocolate pie. When one piece is removed, the other pieces ooze towards the open place. Some roles that our beloved child played in the family are slowly assumed by other family members, but not all.

   Mother of sixteen-year-old son killed in truck-car-tractor accident:
   "My surviving children and grandchildren have become very valuable to me. We understand that each time we see each other could be the last. My child was a huggin' child and my other chil-

dren realize I miss that. We all give hugs now."

I sometimes use a family mobile when giving grief talks. To remove one family member throws the whole mobile in disarray, and that's how we are. The family is in a constant flux until we become somewhat stable again. One mother said something that is so true: "Each member of a family becomes a different person than they were before the death of the child. Each one has to do their own grieving in their own way."

2. Not only do we grieve for our child and the future they will never have, but we also grieve for the loss of ourselves, for the person we were. We realize we will never quite be that person again.

Mother of two-year-old son. Four and one-half years since death:

"I feel I have changed so radically. I really mourn what I see as the loss of myself – the funny, innocent, caring, smart, future-oriented me that **was**. I mourn my child, but I also mourn the loss of **my life** too."

However, grief does soften and mellow with time if we work with time. This young mother likely *will* find happiness again, only in different ways.

3. All bereaved parents suffer from extra temporal crisis, or the feeling that our child is not supposed to die before we do. That's just not the way the world works.

To every thing there is a season, and
A time to every purpose under the heaven:
A time to be born, and a time to die...

The Holy Bible, King James Version,

Ecclesiastes 3: 1-2

So, what happened to us? The timing of our child's death is out of sequence, increasing our feelings of unfairness and stress. Add to that the *disconnect* between society's expectations for how we *should* feel and how we *actually* feel, and we're in a real mess.

4. Our future generations were forever altered when our child died. If it was our only child, it is the *end of the line* for us.

Mother of thirty-one year-old daughter killed in auto accident (Eighteen months from death until survey):

"[I have] the sense that all was/is/will be for naught. My child's death gives me no future – meaning my future derived from my past, who my grand-mother was, mother is, and myself, now stops. I will never be a grandparent. My place in the line has ended."

Older parents and parents whose child was an only child seem to deal more with issues of generativity than do younger parents and parents with surviving children.

5. We may see the world differently than we did prior to our child's death.

Mother of 18-year-old son killed in accident three years prior to survey:

"I'm different. I don't fit in. Living only for myself and not thinking it's right. Trying to enjoy life, yet not happy. Repeating myself. Retreating–don't want to leave home for great, lengthy periods–almost get ill. Yet, I force myself to do activities."

Mother of ten-year-old daughter killed by drunk driver 27 months prior to survey:

"I seem to experience life on a different plane. Sometimes what goes on here doesn't seem real."

6. Regardless of how our child died, his/her death will always be a **time marker** in our lives. Just as we have *Before Christ* and *After Christ*, we now have *Before our Child's Death* and *After our Child's Death*. Later, when we try to remember when something happened, it is always "Let's see now...that must be in the early '80's, because it was before Joe's death." Our child's death is a reference point in time for us as long as we live.

Before and After

Before, we thought we knew the kind of world we lived in. We believed that if we were good people and tried to be the best parents we could be, everything would be OK. *After*, we realized that we lived in a different reality, one we knew little about. We didn't even know that there could be such a thing as *after* until it happened to our family. We didn't know that for us, *before* was already over. Our whole lives changed in a second, and we never saw it coming.

Charlene Cole

Despite the heartaches of early bereavement, it **is** possible for us to work through the terrible times and be stronger and wiser, and quite possibly even happier than ever before. We learn what is really important in life and to live as we have never lived before. We will always miss our child, we will always have hard times, but we <u>can</u> find happiness again. We have to remember that when we exit one doorway, we're entering another. It's a new life, a scary one at first, but it can be very good.

Chapter IX
Stigmatized Deaths

Many of our childrens deaths carry a note of stigma, or a mark of shame that is placed by society on the death. These include nearly all deaths, but especially AIDS, Autoerotic Asphyxiation, drug overdose, suicide, homicide, SIDS, and even accidental death, especially if risk-taking behavior was involved. Acquaintances and friends don't know how to approach the subject of our child's death - so they don't. We often feel very alone in our grief.

In stigmatized deaths, we often feel tainted and blameworthy. No matter how many good works we have accomplished in the past, no matter how good a parent we were to our child, we somehow feel that if we had been better parents, our child would be alive. Unfortunately, our friends and family may feel the same way, which certainly adds to our grief. Sometimes we're left out of social activities, or, if we are invited, we might be avoided or shunned once we are there. What bothers me the most is to have a friend rave on about her wonderful, over-achieving son or daughter, knowing that my only child is dead. Even though I know that she is *assuring herself* that my misfortune could never happen to her, it still hurts.

Why do people do this? It is normal to fear the unknown and to find reasons why something bad has happened to someone else - not us. The *just world assumption* is the belief that the world is a just and fair place; therefore, victims of misfortune must have done something to deserve their fate. We get what we deserve and deserve what we get. Through our misfortune, we know this is not true. It is simply an *illusion* of control that helps people feel safer in their world.

We often receive unhelpful advice: "It's time to move on." Or, "Looks like a support group would bring you down, rather than help." On this subject, one of my closest friends said, "Well, I guess misery loves company."

When I look back, I realize that I often felt that I was being discussed behind my back – my parenting style, my relationship with my son, and what I could have done differently. Maybe not, but I felt that way. After doing research for this chapter, I now realize that these thoughts are normal for stigmatized deaths. [1]

Chapter X
Mothers and Fathers Grief

The battle of the sexes will never be won...
There's too much fraternizing with the enemy!
Author Unknown

We are so different in every other way, why do we think we will grieve alike? Do men and women always agree on movies or TV programs? Do we shop alike? Often a man goes into a store for a particular item, buys it, and leaves. Women may go *shopping*, come home with five or six items...minus the one thing we intended to buy. I was told, by a man of course, that men attack problems with a single-minded purpose while women do a million things at once. *We call it multi-tasking!*

"There are two kinds of people at parties - those who want to go home early, and those who want to be the last ones in the place. The trouble is that they're usually married to each other."
...Author Unknown

When writing these opening paragraphs, I asked my brother what he and his wife do that is totally different. He said (after fifty years of marriage), "The only thing Sue and I do **alike** is maybe open a pickle jar the same way," and so it is with many of us. Unfortunately, society often believes that since we lost the same child, our grief will be the same, and we'll be supportive of each other. Sometimes this is true, often not. Just because we have another person in the house does not mean we are sharing.

In the first place, grief is an individual thing, and no one, even our spouse, can do our grieving for us. It is our own individual Hell. Even though we may *want* to be there for each other, it is difficult to help another when we are in so much pain ourselves. As one mother stated: "After all, you can't lean on a tree that's already splintered."

I would have thought that Gene and I would grieve *somewhat* alike. No way! I talked and talked. He was quiet. I reached out in all directions for help. He kept his grief inside. I was Joe's mother, he was Joe's stepfather – *how could he possibly have loved him as much?* Thank God, I never said that, but sometimes I thought it. He later led workshops for stepparents and apparently, really helped them. I now know that stepparents are often the forgotten grievers. Gene and I did eventually learn that just because we were handling our grief differently did not mean that either of us was *wrong,* it simply meant that we were grieving in our own individual ways. *We get in trouble when we expect our mate's grief to mirror our own.*

So many factors determine how we grieve that it is no wonder that we handle our grief so differently. For one thing, our individual *personalities* greatly influence how we grieve. If one of us is an introvert and the other an extrovert, we do not change when tragedy strikes. Both of us will grieve, but each in our own way.

Mother of twenty-year-old son, fifteen months since accident:

"I'm a very private person, and I grieve privately. My husband grieves more openly, but then, he is a more outward, emotional person. I think that grieving is not a male-female difference as much as a personality difference."

Different *cultures* express grief in various ways and have different grieving traditions. A friend of mine worked in Taiwan when she was young She said that a young man in her office had beautiful flowing hair, but he came in one day with a horrible buzz cut; he was almost bald. She was horrified until she learned that this was a Taiwanese custom for someone who had suffered a significant loss. It served as a reminder that, just as the hair will grow, grief will heal. His short haircut let others know that he had suffered a loss; then, as his hair grew, others would know that he was a little further along in his grief journey.

A little closer to home, some families prefer to *keep it in*, while others reach out in all directions for help. If we are brought up one way, it is difficult to suddenly change. I have attempted to reach out to newly bereaved parents who told me that they prefer to "keep it in the family, handle it themselves." I respect that. Different family backgrounds definitely influence how a person grieves. The *rub* comes in when one of us grew up one way, and our partner grew up another.

Previous loss experiences influences how we cope with our child's death. In my research, I found that young parents have a particularly difficult time. They have not experienced the usual gradual increase in losses: pets, grandparents, then possibly parents, and/or mates. To be thrown into the extreme depths of parental bereavement is totally devastating. There are many reasons why young parents have a difficult time, but on the bright side, my research also indicated that younger parents tend to *bounce back* quicker than some of us oldies.

We may be surprised that what brings comfort to our partner may totally devastate us; on the other hand, what helps us may cause them pain.

Mother:

"Church, music, faith have been a comfort to him – and my time of greatest pain. We go to church–he finds comfort and 'communion' with our son–I feel anguish."

Mother of twenty-two-year-old son:

"I need to talk a lot. He doesn't. I need a spirituality and am searching different religions and other paths...My spouse is angry at religion and thinks God is useless. I need tangible stuff – pictures, candles, flowers at cemetery, etc., - Husband needs other things."

Like it or not, *gender* does appear to influence how we grieve. The tendency for mothers to be more verbal and expressive about grief than fathers was stressed by both mothers and fathers in the survey. The following statements are typical of **many** in the sample.

Mother:

"I want to talk about our son all the time, but I cry–so my husband walks away. I think he feels that if he doesn't talk about it, it never happened."

Father:

"My wife needs to talk about our child's death. I prefer to listen to other grieving parents, but I do not talk much about my feelings."

Mother:

"He never wanted to talk about our son while

I couldn't do anything but talk. Every time Jeff's name was mentioned, my husband would leave the room."

While the mother's verbalization and the father's lack of expression sometimes created problems, this was not always true.

Mother:

"I talk non-stop and he listens. I started to worry that I wasn't allowing him to verbalize because I was always talking. We discussed this, and he told me that he is glad when I talk, because many times, I verbalize for him what he isn't able to do. His grief is so great and private that he just keeps it to himself.

Over the past two years, he does talk more (by that, I mean initiate the conversation,) but, for the most part, I'm the one who talks my emotions 'out'."

Sometimes the father was the more expressive of the two.

Father:

"I want to talk about my grief and feelings to my spouse. My spouse does not want to talk to me about her feelings."

Men seem to have a more difficult time finding helpful, listening friends than women. An interesting piece of research I discovered was on the different *conversational styles* of men and women. Apparently women typically use a more *enabling* style of conversation that tends to initiate a response. We acknowledge our friend's comment, express agreement, and are usually supportive of her viewpoint. As a result, our friend feels that we understand her pain. [1 (p. 517)]

Men, in contrast, tend to use a more restrictive style of conversation that *informs* and *expresses ideas*, rather than sharing *feelings*. Unfortunately, this conversational style often shortens or misdirects the conversation, bringing it to an end. Consequently, men may have a more difficult time finding good *listening* friends. [2 (pp. 513-520)] Whether this is due to cultural, genetic, or a combination of influences, I'm not sure.

> **Father** of seventeen-year-old-daughter, killed in
> accident five years prior to survey:
>> "Wife: Anger at God
>>   Talks to friend
>> Me: No anger at God
>>   Have no friend who understands."

We tend to grieve in ways that is expected by society because this is what has been modeled and reinforced throughout our life. Fathers have traditionally assumed the roles of family protector, provider, and problem solver, one in control of all situations. [3 (p. 62); 4 (p. 27); 5 (p. 27)] When a problem arises, a solution should be found, the problem **fixed**. However, there is no way to fix this problem, to bring back the dead child. The father is suddenly catapulted into a new reality; he has been presented with an unpreventable, unsolvable problem of such magnitude that it threatens to disrupt the entire family.

Father:

> "Used to think that if you were a good per-
> son, God would protect you. Not true. Thought

70

I could solve any problem within the family. Not true. Thought we were a close family that could handle any problem together. Not true, all grieve differently, like four people, each in his/her own corner. Thought I was strong. Not true – cried a lot. Thought I could wait for things. Not true – NOW is important. Tomorrow may not come."

Failure to control life's events and prevent the child's death may leave both parents questioning their abilities as parents. However, for the father, his sense of failure coupled with the cultural need to present strong, stoic images may prevent him from openly expressing his feelings, even with his mate. Unfortunately, the mother may then believe *He's not grieving as much as I; he must not have loved the child as much.* However, the father may simply be trying to survive himself and/or to shield his partner from pain. He may be thinking *Woman! Leave me alone and let me grieve in my own way.*

The younger generation of boys and men tend to be more open, more expressive and more willing to share their emotions than in generations past. Also, since a larger number of women have careers and work outside the home, men usually take a more active role in the care of home and children. This generational difference is expressed by the following **mother**, an active leader in The Compassionate Friends.

"I watch the men in our support group. The younger ones–under thirty-five share more easily and do better–cry openly. The older ones have just been taught differently. Once I learned to accept this vast difference, I was able to let go of my anger towards my husband."

71

Communication problems may drive a psychological wedge between the two parents, leaving each more alone. Either partner who previously looked towards his/her spouse for support may now feel totally isolated and alone, not realizing that his/her spouse is also immersed in the unfathomable depths of parental grief.

> Many marriages would be better if the
> husband and wife clearly understood
> they're on the same side.
>
> Zig Ziglar

Sometimes a *balance* occurs in marriages after the death of a child. If one partner cries, the other shows less effect. If one does not acknowledge the loss, the other reacts more intensely.

Mother:
"My husband took our daughter's death very hard. He was the type of father to our three girls that was always there for them. He played with them when they were small. We even still took all vacations together, summer and winter, even though two were married ...I could not share my grief in front of him. He would get so upset and say he couldn't handle it."

As parents, we each had a very special and unique relationship with our child, unlike any other. Consequently, the grief we now experience and the manner in which we express our grief may be similar, yet totally different for each of us. One result is that we have different *triggers* that "set us off."

Father:

"The basic difference now, after two and one/ half years, is in the trigger mechanisms. She can see food in the supermarket that our son liked, and it brings her to tears. I'll be doing some work, run across something that Mark had his name on, and I'll respond tearfully."

Mothers are often more involved in their children's daily routines and activities than fathers. For her to smell remnants of cologne or powder, or to suddenly have to set the table for one less are likely typical everyday reminders that she encounters on a daily basis. These can be very painful because they are the least expected. A typical trigger for mothers revolves about food.

The Cabbage Core

Last Sunday, we were having a happy family dinner at my sister-in-law's home, just as we do quite often. We all filled our plates and were having a really good day. I filled my bowl with boiled cabbage, like I always do and had eaten all of it, except the core. I was sort of pushing it around in the bowl without thinking while I was talking to my brother-in-law about our plans for a garden this spring. My husband, Eric, made the comment, "Hey! How did you get my cabbage core!? E. C. and I used to fight over it every Sunday. Remember?" Well! That just hit me like a ton of bricks. I burst into tears and cried for the longest time. Eric was apologizing for his comment, my daughter was hugging me tight, and my sister-in-law was just silent. When I told her later what had happened, she and I cried some more. Then, we were all better for a while.

By Jeanne Hoelle
In loving memory of E. C. Hoelle (Forever 17)

In addition to likely having more *triggers*, a mother may feel very lonely after the loss of her child if her social network was basically her family.

Mother:

"We both express our grief openly with each other but my spouse has a career to return to which is useful as a distraction. My 'career' was motherhood, and I am left confronting the loss on a more constant level."

Mothers often have a "symbiotic attachment" to their children that begins with conception and lessens with birth, growth, and development. A special bond and closeness may remain throughout life because of "one identity" beginnings, a time when a mother's body is shared with her child. [3] (p 70)

Father:

"My wife's identity was closely knit with our daughter. My wife brought her forth and poured her life into her. She has more guilt feelings (not awakening in time) while I have more feelings of helplessness."

Employment may provide opportunities and/or pitfalls for us, depending on our employment role and co-worker relationships.

The death of a child often lowers our self-esteem by increasing our sense of failure - we failed to prevent the tragedy. Employment may help us feel productive and useful again, as well as give us brief respites from grief.

Returning to work seemed to be therapeutic for some parents, almost impossible for others, and serve as an escape from grief for still others.

Father:

"It hit her sudden and for a long time, for six months she was unable to work. My grief was less sudden, and work was part of my release."

Father:

"My wife grieved very deeply from the beginning and worked through her grief in 2–3 years. I stuffed my grief and buried myself in my job. I didn't work through my grief completely until I joined TCF nine years later."

Mother:

"He wanted to be home more. I wanted to keep busy and run. He expressed his feelings to everyone. I put on my public face. He cut back on his working hours and retired."

The stress and grief after the death of a child is tragically overwhelming, and the following couples were really struggling.

Mother:

"My spouse is a very quiet person and does not

talk about our son at all. After three years, we do not communicate at all. We just live in the same house."

Mother:

"My husband is fifty-six, I am fifty-five. We've been married thirty-two years, but I'm not sure we will survive this. We still don't discuss our only son's death."

Mother:

"He never talks about it. I have to cry private-ly. We lash out at each other in our grief...Since last November's trial [malpractice], my spouse has been enraged, and I am depressed. We are at a bad place in our fifty-year marriage. Our coun-selor is helping us sort it out. Wish us luck. We want to stay married."

The chances of any two people in the world grieving alike is slim to none; therefore, we might as well accept the fact that our spouse's grief will be somewhat, or entirely different than our own. The following couples seem to have accepted this fact.

Mother:

"I had to search for many answers to my unan-swered questions. I had no experience with death before our son was killed. I was very lost and confused, in addition to coming to terms with the death. I read a lot, talked to many people, trying to find answers. My husband was patient and under-standing and we have worked hard to support and respect each other's grief work."

Father:

"I like to be alone with my thoughts, to cry or not cry. My wife likes to have me around on those days she's feeling down – and if she's down – now we're both down. But, I realize that we married 'for better or worse,' and losing a child has got to be the worse."

Grief is as individual as a fingerprint, and we each have to find ways to take care of ourselves. Sometimes what works for one doesn't work for the other.

Father:

"My wife is an introvert and at first had a hard time expressing her feelings about the death of our son. It was very hard for her to talk, cry or express any emotion about his death. I became depressed and once [I] realized this, began a work out program and started training for a triathlon that I completed six months after.

Our time line on how we have progressed through the grief stages has been very different, and the one thing that saved our marriage was realizing that we were grieving differently."

Mother:

"He finds Scott, our son who died, in his mountain walks, while hunting, while fishing, while computer programming, etc. He is not a good communicator; he is an analytical thinker (chemist), and we do not communicate as well as we should – but enough – to help with others in TCF, as well as our own. Most of all, **it is alright to grieve separately!"**

Not only does **our** personality, past history and other variables influence how we grieve, but also our **child's** personality, the roles he or she played in our life, the ambivalence of our relationship, the cause and **perceived** preventability of their death, his or her age – there are so many factors that influence how we grieve that it is no wonder that husbands and wives seldom grieve alike or on the same time lines.

In conclusion, if we need to talk, and our partner will not, perhaps we can find a caring, supportive friend. However, no matter how much our friends love us, they tend to eventually think *enough is enough*! That is why support groups are so beneficial. We all understand. We understand totally *bizarre* behavior, because we have all been there.

However, if you're not comfortable going to a support group, that's OK too. If you are reading this book, you're doing your grief work in YOUR way, your time, and that's what we all have to do.

Suggestions for better communication between spouses:
(Some of these are from a handout given at the 1991 The Compassionate Friends Conference by Joe & Elizabeth Rousseau. Some are from various family counseling classes and seminars.)
1. Make your marriage a top priority so that the loss of your child does not become a double loss. If you're at a real impasse with your spouse and he/she is agreeable, marriage and family counseling can be very helpful.

2. Resolve to *have fun* at least two hours a week with your spouse or your entire immediate family.

3. Do unexpected kindnesses for your spouse.

4. Use the old and trusted "I feel" method of communication. "I feel _____ when you_____. I would like for us/you to _____." Examples of *feeling* words may be *frustrated, angry, hurt, fearful*. Example: "I feel frustrated and hurt when you walk out of the room when I mention *Jennifer*'s name. We both loved her so much, and I want us to be able to talk about our pain and feelings together." If he/she simply cannot do that, then find a friend, support group or counselor for yourself. Your spouse may be dealing with his/her loss the only way he can at the moment.

5. Practice your counseling skills. (A) Listen, (B) clarify.....repeat what they said in your words. Use silence to encourage them to talk, express their feelings. Ask questions pertaining to what they said. Be supportive and understanding, just as you would with a friend.

6. **Never hit below the belt** by bringing up things from the past that you know will hurt him/her.

7. Do not **gunny-sack** resentments. Eventually the bag of resentments becomes so full that it explodes.

8. *Touch* dissipates anger. Try holding hands when you talk.

9. Recognize and compliment the positives in your spouse.

10. Above all, remember that you and your spouse will very likely grieve differently, have different time lines, different *triggers*, and that's okay.

For My Hero

When our son died, I thought
You would hold me and comfort me
And make everything right
Like you always did.

You never let me down before.
When you couldn't fix things,
I was furious with you.
You wouldn't even talk or cry
Or throw things
Like I did.

When you didn't grieve my way,
The right way, I thought
You loved him less
And said so.

Now I know you didn't let me down.
You cried, you cared, you did the best
That any man in pain could do.
And I forgive you
For not being Superman
Or me.

Pat Dyson

Chapter XI
When Will the Pain End?
and
Finding Happiness Again

Early on, I asked every bereaved parent I knew, "How long will it take? Will I ever be happy again?" They usually just hugged me, and, with a sad little smile, said "It just takes time." However, with the passage of time, the prospect of ever being happy again looked quite bleak. Finally, I reached a point where I could only envision my life as being an endless number of pain-filled days and felt much like the author of the following poem.

> Once I wanted total happiness,
> Now, I will settle for a little less pain.
>   ...Ashleigh Brilliant
>   TCF Newsletter

However, the wheel of life did not stop at my lowest ebb; it kept turning. I remember hearing speakers and reading articles that offered **hope**. I distinctly remember Darcie Sims (professional speaker) saying "Survival isn't enough; I want to **live!**" I thought "**Yes!**" Then, in a smaller voice, I questioned, "*How do I do that?*"

I grabbed onto that parcel of hope, wondering if happiness was a thing of my past, or if it actually could be a possibility for my future. If so, **when**, as if happiness was on a time line, an all-or-nothing condition. I would be miserable, then, suddenly, happiness would return? A little poem in a TCF newsletter caught my attention.

Just for Today

Just for today
I will be happy!
Just for today
I will search for and find
A new beauty to gladden my heart,
As in the days of my long ago.

Just for today
I will put yesterday with its pain behind me
And bask in the warmth of today.
I will lift up my eyes to sunshine,
Let my fingertips touch
The glad rays of a new day.
My peace shall not be of Yesterday
or Tomorrow,
My peace shall be of Today!

- Author Unknown–

I realized that I might not be happy for a whole day, or a whole hour – or even for a whole minute at that point, but I could grasp *seconds* of joy. Surely I could do that.

Then, a very small thing happened that added credence to my new realization. While I was standing at my kitchen window washing dishes, a beautiful cardinal landed on my window sill. It was so close that I could have touched its scarlet feathers, were it not for the glass. I felt utter joy at its beauty. I think that is the first time that I had actually felt joy without having the background shadow of pain since Joe's death. It was such a magnificent feeling, even if it was for just a couple of seconds. But, it was a start.

A small article entitled *The Station*, by Ralph J. Hastings, says that we are so often bent on reaching the station in life or some end goal, that we miss the **trip**. We do not do that as much any more, do we? We value the sunrise, the feeling of wet grass between our toes, the sound of our loved-one's voice. We treasure the moment, rather than planning for a happy *someday*.

> "…If I had my life to live over…there would have been more 'I love yous' and more 'I'm sorrys'…but mostly, I would seize every minute, look at it, and really see it, and never give it back."
>
> Erma Bombeck
> Andrews McMeel Publishing

Not only do we become more aware of each moment, but we also have greater capacity for joy and happiness. Due to the depths of darkness we have experienced, our glimpses of sunlight seem so much brighter, so much more beautiful.

> "The deeper that sorrow carves into your being,
> The more joy you can contain."
>
> Kahlil Gibran
> *The Prophet*

Yes, we do find happiness again, but, we have to work for it. We have to work through our grief, and at the same time, grab onto every moment of laughter, joy, excitement and feelings of love that we can find.

So, "How long will the pain last?" Of course, there is no set answer. Even though our child died, the love we had for him/her did not. We often hear, "Grief is the price we pay for love," and it is true. Grief is nature's way of healing a psychological wound or amputation. While there will always be remnants of pain, the pain softens and mellows. We learn to treasure our child's life, rather than dwelling on his/her death.

We have exited the doorway to our treasured past, and for this, we mourn. We will miss our child, and he or she will be a part of us forever, but new joys, new people, new interests enter our lives, giving us the potential for new happiness.

However, we must remember that we do not reap and sow in the same day. Nor does time alone heal our broken hearts; we must work with time. All those painful emotions - anger, guilt, fear, loneliness - must be worked through, bit by bit, or perhaps, tear by tear. Finally, one day, we find that we not only want to *survive*, we want to *live*. Just like Darcie Sims said! We realize that, yes, yesterday *is* gone, but today is a whole new day. Life *will* be good again. Just hang on tight to your friends and family for support and have faith that life will again bring hope, joy, and peace.

Just as the ancient mythical Phoenix arose from the ashes of ruin, we too can emerge from grief as stronger, more compassionate and caring individuals. And, like the Phoenix, we are *different* people now, but we have a new inner beauty and strength we did not possess before. Our child's **death** taught us so much about **life**, and for this, as with so many things, we thank them.

Before It's Too Late
If I should wake up
On a soft summer morning
With only one day left to live,
I'd cherish the moments
And notice each color;

84

I'd give all the love I could give …

If I had just twenty-four hours for living,
Things that don't matter could wait;
I'd play with the children
And hear all their stories;
I'd tell you "I love you"
Before it's too late …

I'd light one small candle
To brighten the darkness,
To shine in the heart of my friend;
I'd take time to notice
The view from my window,
I'd walk in my garden again …

If I had just twenty-four hours for living,
Things that don't matter could wait;
I'd play with the children
And hear all their stories;
I'd tell YOU "I love you"
Before it's too late.

Author Unknown

Chapter XII
Gifts from our Child

**Should you shield the canyons from the
windstorms, you would never see
the beauty of their carvings.
Favorite quote of Elisabeth Kübler-Ross**

You and I have known windstorms in our lives, haven't we? But just as the windstorms left beautiful carvings in the canyons, the windstorms in our lives can also leave beautiful gifts for us. However, we have a choice whether or not we accept these gifts. Kübler-Ross said, "Out of every tragedy can come a blessing or a curse, compassion or bitterness - the choice is yours". [1] (p. 49)

* Original painting by Charlene Cole

I am not saying that we can choose not to hurt, because that is not a possibility. We have to walk with the pain to ever get to the other side. We have been subjected to the depths of Hell, but with time, we start to climb out of this seemingly bottomless pit and actually have hopes for tomorrow. We eventually realize that precious gifts await us *because* of our suffering. Of course, we would definitely rather have our child back, but we do not have that choice.

> The oyster tries to expel the sand and grit:
> When it cannot, it makes a pearl.
> Author Unknown

What are these gifts? You know them as well as I do, and these are only a few.

1. Our first gift is our greater realization of the preciousness and brevity of life. One searing moment ended our child's life and changed our life forever. Perhaps if a car had been traveling one second faster or slower, a wreck would not have occurred, or had the trajectory of a bullet been a fraction of an inch to the left or right, it would not have hit a vital organ, or had we awakened one hour sooner... Unfortunately these things did not happen, and we now better understand our vulnerability to disaster and the preciousness of each and every moment.

Mother, five years after death of daughter:
"'The Meaning of Life' is life itself...a breath, a heartbeat; how precious from beginning to end."

Father, sixteen years after death of daughter:
"Life hangs by a thin, narrow thread. I never thought about this before."

There are so many moments in our yesterday that we would give anything - certainly our life - to relive, but we can not. Joe used to embarrass me because he seemed to gobble down a hamburger in two bites. Wouldn't I love to see him do that now? I would not fuss! Why did I not realize what a precious gift I had when I had it? We would all love to relive moments from our yesterday, and actually, this may be one thing that moves us forward, making us forever see the small, inconsequential joys in our life *today* that we once took for granted. Sorrow has sharpened our senses. We now understand the brevity of life and how one fleeting second can change our world forever.

> It's not how long we live that's important,
> But how deeply we savor the moment.
>> John Claypool

2. Our priorities return to the basics: family and friends rather than material possessions, and God's creations rather than man's inventions; these become our new priorities. Before our child(ren) died, we certainly would have said that the most important thing in our life was our family. We would say this as we were working overtime, or cleaning the house before guests were to arrive, or whatever. Now, the dishes and house can wait. The work will still be there tomorrow. We spend time with those we love and say, "I love you" before it's too late.

Parents in the survey nearly all expressed sentiments like those expressed by the following mothers:

Six years since death of daughter:
"Treasure each family member more and tell

88

them often, love them freely and openly – don't be afraid of tenderness and emotional displays."

Three years since death of child:
"Little things, like flat tires, broken appliances …they're such little things. Now, my other two children are more important, or I should say, I'm <u>aware</u> they're more important."

Four years and eight months since death of daughter:
"Life is so precious. The little things that people get so upset about are really nothing at all. Children are more special than ever, whether they are what everyone thinks of as 'normal' or not."

3. We have greater compassion for all suffering human beings and animals. Since we have known the depths of pain, we better understand the pain of others and want to be there for them.

To ease another's heartache is to forget one's own.

Abe Lincoln

Many parents reinvest time and energy, doing things to help others or to improve the world in honor of their child. We know that every life affects eternity in some way, and we want our child's life to have contributed something positive and special to the world. We do what we can to keep their memory alive.

Mother:
"I'll be a kind ear and warm shoulder to anyone beginning their grief journey – a stepping stone.

Come, take my hand. It's all right. I understand."

Mother:

"Do what you can, when you can, where you are. Do good in your child's name, if for no other reason. Help others and be helpful to others."

Following is a poem written by St. Teresa of Avila centuries ago:

Christ has No body on earth but yours;
No hands but yours;
No feet but yours;
Yours are the eyes
Through which He is to look out
Christ's compassion to the world:
Yours are the feet
With which He is to go about doing good;
Yours are the hands
With which he is to bless now.

We find that by helping others, we help ourselves.

4. We have a greater inner strength than ever before. If I can survive this, by golly, I can survive anything. We may be thrown off by some minor problem that causes us a temporary setback, but for the most part, we're so much stronger in all the ways that count.

I remember a story about a woman who treasured a certain piece of pottery in her home. One day, a strong wind blew the precious piece over and shattered it into seemingly hundreds of pieces. The lady cried, then slowly began picking up the pieces to throw away, but she could not do it. She carefully put them into a bag ... for what purpose, she did not know. Then one day she pulled the dusty bag from the top of her closet and slowly started gluing pieces back together, piece by piece. She had to wait for the glued pieces to dry before she could add more. Then, finally, one day long after the treasured piece of pottery had broken, she glued in the final piece. It could never be as it had been before, but it was stronger than ever before. Just as the glued-together piece of pottery had seams, we now have scars, but we do feel stronger, wiser, and more compassionate than ever before.

Mother of ten-year-old daughter:

"I have grown in ways that I never dreamed. I am sorry that it took my daughters death to make me stronger, but I am glad I have grown. It will be seven years this October since Jennifer died. It has been an on-going process of growth. It's been long and painful, but I'm glad I'm in a position to help others now."

5. We often have less fear of our own death. Whether it is because we hope to be reunited with our child, or that we see death as a quiet transition from one plane to another, death is less fearful.

Mother:

"I no longer fear death. My surviving children and grandchildren have become very valuable to me. We have more family get-togethers. We each one understand that each time we see each other could be the last ...We say 'I love you' often and give hugs all the time."

Mother of twenty-six-year-old son:

"Death is no longer fearful – the time we have on earth is so short that we now try to make the most of everyday and everything."

Mother of eighteen-year-old daughter:

"I no longer have any concerns about my death except that I wouldn't want it to be before my children are grown because I wouldn't want to be the cause of additional suffering for them. I view death as the reconciliation with my child whom I miss so terribly and yearn to hold so much."

However, we may truly believe that we do not fear death... until it threatens. My friend, Georgia, was having a difficult time and went to visit mutual friends who lived on a nearby polo ranch. Randy, a crusty ole cowboy, asked her to go feed the ponies and drive around the ranch with him. Fresh air would be good for her. Once in the pickup, she broke down and kept repeating, "I just don't want to live anymore – I want to die! There's nothing to live for." With a mischievous gleam in his eye, Randy saw his chance. He rammed the old pickup into gear, put the pedal to the metal and headed straight for the edge of a cliff. Georgia panicked and screamed "STOP! STOP! Let me OUT! NOW!"

Of course, Randy did stop – right at the edge of the cliff. "Georgia, I thought you said you wanted to die!"

When she recovered, she meekly said..."Well, maybe just not quite yet!"

I can remember having similar sentiments. Once, when I

was snow-skiing, I stopped at the top of the mountain literally scared to death. I had been sure that I had absolutely no fear of death, so why was I so afraid? My brother eventually had to gently coax me down the hill.

6. Our child's death is often a catalyst for value changes – and that is not a bad thing. One area that is often thrown into total chaos - necessitating a complete overhaul - is religion.

While the survey asked no direct question pertaining to religion, so many parents wrote about their religious struggles that it is apparently a *hot subject* for most of us. Support groups generally discourage any discussion pertaining to religion or politics, so where do we turn?

Most of the responses pertaining to religion resulted from the following question: "Have your views about life changed since the death of your child? If so, what are some of these changes?" I was surprised that religion was the main topic discussed. Following is a **small** sampling of the responses.

**Mother, two years and two months since
the death of nineteen-year-old son:**
      "When [my son] died, I began to question it all and to question my beliefs and priorities in my own life. I was spinning in chaos and could trust nothing I had previously believed without thorough investigation."

**Mother, thirty-two months after death of
twenty-six-year-old daughter:**
      "My religious beliefs have been absolutely challenged. I do not blindly believe, or have 'unwavering faith'. I still have days where I feel anger towards God. However, the anger is more placid,

93

and I don't think about the 'why's' anymore."

**Mother, one year and eight months after
death of twenty-four-year-old son:**

"My spiritual belief system was shattered by
his death. I see my former beliefs as simplistic
and childlike and hope that I can grow into a stronger, more mature faith."

By questioning our previous religious beliefs, we often develop a deeper understanding of what we DO believe. Or, do not.

**Mother of nineteen-year-old son.
Four and one-half years since death:**

"I realized that God does not take. He gave
us the free will to interact with others. With that,
we pay the consequences. We and other human
beings make mistakes. Sometimes we live with
them. Sometimes we die with them."

**Mother of nineteen-year-old, one year
and two months since death:**

"I believe in an intelligence or higher power
to the universe, but not a Santa Claus who gives
and withholds, rewards and punishes. If I thought
God had anything to do with my son's death, then
I would want to be an atheist. If I thought that
God even sat by idly while my son died and did
nothing when he could have done something, then
I would hate that God. I don't believe it though –
and more than ever, I am now convinced that the
compassionate nature of God is through us human

94

beings. God does not pull the strings – we pull our own strings and choose to expand or contract, to love or not."

Mother of two children killed in auto accident:

"I believe that God does not *take* our child, but is there to comfort, to heal bereaved parents - if we will be healed. He gave us freedom and that freedom is awesome, for it not only frees us to life and growth, but it also frees us to death and destruction as a result of our own doings – or the doings of others."

The faith of some parents was strengthened, while other parents became more spiritual or shunned organized religion altogether.

Mother of ten-year-old daughter,
Almost seven years since death:

"I have become closer to my Lord and Savior, Jesus Christ. That poem about 'footprints' is very true. He has carried me until I was able to walk by myself with help.

When I worked for Hospice, we found that a person may be deeply spiritual, yet had never set foot in a church. Many participants in the survey leaned towards spirituality, rather than organized religion.

Mother, six years since death:

"Organized religion makes me mad. My relationship with God is very personal now. I used to be very religious – or let's say – I was involved in religion. Not now."

Some parents lost their faith altogether. In talking about the differences between mothers and fathers, one mother said "My husband has made few major decisions in his life, and I can tell you, he will never waiver on his stand. One [decision] is that he [now] firmly believes there is no God."

I am espousing no religious faith or belief system. I am simply saying it is okay and normal to question our beliefs after the death of a child.

"God made so many different kinds of people. Why would he allow only one way to serve Him?"

Martin Buber

For years after Joe's death, I would be on time everywhere but church. There was no way I could arrive at church on time. An article in a TCF newsletter entitled "Hidden Anger Checklist" brought to my attention that consistently being late was a sign of hidden anger; then I understood. I was mad at God, and, boy, would I show Him by being late! Silly? Yes, but unconsciously, maybe this is what I was doing.

We often frighten our friends, family and religious community with our *Search for Meaning* in our child's death. We delve into our previous religious beliefs, and this may be very disturbing to them. After a Compassionate Friends Conference, one of my friends asked if I thought the conference had helped me. I said, "Yes! One of our main speakers, Dr. John Claypool, talked on *Grief and Religion*, and it was so helpful to me."

She said, "I'm glad, because I've been so worried about your anger towards God and your attitude about religion." I tried to explain that I believe much differently now, but that does not make it bad. To me, my anger and the questioning of my former beliefs was a natural consequence of my losing Joe. Had I not prayed for his safety daily? What happened? How could I **not** question my former beliefs? I now believe that by questioning and examining our beliefs, we develop a deeper understanding of what we truly do believe. We may develop a deeper faith than ever before – although perhaps a different faith. We may become more spiritual, have different beliefs, or lose our faith altogether. We seem to travel down different paths and arrive at different destinations in our spiritual journeys, - on different time lines - and that's OK.

7. A very important gift from our child is the gift of unconditional and unlimited love we knew because our child lived. We are much like the Velveteen Rabbit in the children's book who was made real because of the child's love. We learned so much from our child, and we grew in ways we never could have grown without their love and our love for them.

8. The last gift, the most wonderful gift, was our child's life. After their death, we were so consumed with the *why's* - "Why my child? Why did he die?" We finally replace this with prior questions: "Why did he live? What did I ever do to deserve his birth, his love?" We cease wondering why a miracle could not have happened to save our child, as we realize that the miracle is that our child lived at all.

Part 2:
Unique Grief Characteristics
Resulting from Different Types of Death:

Is the grief we feel after the death of a child different from the grief that results from other losses? Most of us believe it is much more severe and long-lasting. However, the *way* our child died can also produce very unique grief characteristics. Following are different types of death and *some* of the unique grief characteristics often felt by parents with each type of death.

Chapter XIII
Miscarriage, Stillbirth,
And Early Infant Death

Those we have held in our arms
For a little while,
We hold in our hearts forever.

Author Unknown

The grief of miscarriage, stillbirth and early infant death may be one of society's least understood and most denied. The mistaken belief that *It was too young for you to really know* does not take into account the cherished hopes and dreams you had for your child, the cheerfully decorated nursery that is now standing empty, or the broken-hearted sisters, brothers, and grandparents that eagerly awaited your new arrival.

Friends may stay away, thinking you need time to heal. Like most people, they do not know what to say unless they have been there. It is a lonely loss.

Erratic hormone shifts and post-partum depression are normal for any mother after a birth; however, when she comes home with *empty arms*, her grief may really be intensified. She carried the baby, felt its movements and likely bonded more with the baby than did the father, so sometimes, it is difficult for him to understand her strong grief reactions.

Mother:

"Our first two daughters were stillborn. After

99

the birth of my third daughter, I was told that what happened before was in the past and no longer exists in our lives. That is still how it is for him."

Mother (three miscarriages):

"I don't think it seemed as real to him since he didn't see or hold the babies, so it didn't affect him as much. He's tended to 'put it away.' He doesn't talk to me as much about it as I do with him."

On the other hand, fathers are often neglected. Everyone asks him "How's your wife?" when he is in pain himself. He had probably visualized the good times he and his son would have together...some day. He had plans for that baby too.

I did suffer a miscarriage long ago. At the time, it seemed a blessing because I was trying to leave my abusive first husband, but after Joe's death, I grieved this loss and what might have been. I realize this is not the same as your grief, where you looked forward to and planned for your baby.

What helps?

Grieve in your own way for as long as necessary. Discuss your feelings with a *safe* person you can trust, someone who will listen and *not* try to *take your grief away* by uttering platitudes such as "It was God's will," or "You can have more children." They do this more for themselves anyway. An infant support group might be a real help, as other young mothers or fathers who have experienced the same loss will understand.

"Who, then, can so softly bind
up the wound of
Another as he who has felt

100

the same wound himself?"
Thomas Jefferson

Get the facts. What really happened? What caused the loss? One young mother in the survey did not realize until after their third miscarriage that she could never carry a child to term because of a rare disorder. Above all, do not blame yourself by wondering if you had done things a bit differently, would there have been a different outcome? So, get the facts.

It apparently helps if you were able to hold your infant and say "Goodbye." Photographs also help.

A ceremonial expression of grief is often a comfort. It acknowledges your loss.

Writing your feelings in a journal or diary helps. To help express the raw intensity of your feelings, try poetry. You don't have to follow rules. What you write is for yourself unless you choose to share.

Sometimes love
Is for a moment.
Sometimes love
Is for a lifetime.
Sometimes a moment
Is a lifetime.

Author Unknown

Chapter XIV
SIDS
Sudden Infant Death Syndrome

We cannot, after all, judge a biography by
Its length, by the number of pages in it;
We must judge by the richness of the contents.
...Sometimes the "unfinisheds" are
Among the most beautiful symphonies.

Viktor E. Frankl, M.D.
The Doctor and the Soul

Parents who experience the death of an infant during its first years of life feel that the pain is almost too much to bear, and those whose baby dies from SIDS experience one of the most severe grief reactions of all.[1] The suddenness, the *perceived* preventability, *Why didn't I wake up earlier?*, and the lack of answers complicate an already extremely painful death. Consequently, parents of SIDS babies are thrown into the unfathomable depths of intense mental anguish.

All parents want to know the cause and details of their child's death, even though it is painful to hear and know. However, for the parents of SIDS babies, there are no answers. The parents often feel cheated by the autopsy report, as they hope for a clear, definitive cause of death, but the autopsy finds no cause. When the pathologist can find no indication of a problem sufficient enough to cause death, he/she then certifies that the baby died of SIDS. It does not tell how or why the baby died, it merely excludes all other reasonable explanations.

To complicate matters, SIDS deaths require the involvement of both police and medical experts, and, unfortunately, police are not always trained on how to distinguish between victims of SIDS and victims of abuse. Consequently, the parents may find themselves being treated like criminals when they're already feeling self-reproach. This adds even more anxiety, anger and guilt into the mix, as is evidenced by the following story of a young couple.

Tanya, grandmother of six-month-old Lillie:

"My son, Darin, awakened with a start, instinctively knowing that something was terribly wrong. Lillie had not cried since her mother, Racheal, had breast-fed her and left for work at five-thirty that morning. Terrified, he rushed into her room and immediately realized she wasn't breathing. He frantically started doing CPR and calling 911. Then he called Racheal and me.

I was in Wal-Mart, yelling and screaming over the phone, but no one offered to help. I rushed out and headed for home.

In the meantime, our small town ambulance service came for Lillie, she was transferred to a Sweetwater ambulance in Blackwell, then rushed on to the Sweetwater hospital where the doctors and nurses were anxiously awaiting our Little Lil. I met the ambulance on my way home, made a fast U-turn and followed it to the hospital. They started working on Lillie immediately, but after twenty or thirty minutes, they had to give up.

There were good Samaritans, like Danny Wann from McCoys Funeral Home, that personally drove little Lillie to Dallas for an autopsy. He told us, 'I'll take good care of Lillie and treat her as if she were my own.'

And, there were bad guys as far as I was concerned. The police investigators came to the hospital, separated Darin and Racheal and started interrogating them: 'Did you do drugs or alcohol last night? Did you leave her unattended at any time? Do you have firearms in the home? Could you have caused something to harm her?' On and on.

The hospital had told Darin and Racheal to spend as much time with Little Lil as they wanted, but the investigators ignored that. Darin had to go to the police station for further questioning. Then, Darin and Glenn (Darin's father, my husband) were forced to take the investigators back to Blackwell to search the house. The kids were already traumatized, feeling much self-reproach and guilt, and for the police to treat them like criminals, seemed to me to be the real crime.

When Racheal and Darin were finally allowed to leave, they went to her Dad's house to spend the night. At 11:30 that night, the doorbell rang. It was Child Protective Services, ready to start their investigation. Thankfully, Racheal's father refused to let them in. 'The poor kids have just now settled down. You can come back at a reasonable hour'."

In the first place, as parents, we feel so much responsibility for our child's safety, that when something bad happens, we often believe it must somehow be our fault. For investigators to interrogate the young parents can only strengthen this erroneous belief. Because babies are completely dependent on their parents to meet their every need, the parents develop an overwhelming sense of responsibility. Add to this the high expectations placed on parenthood by society, and parents of SIDS babies often feel they have failed totally and completely at their job.

Tanya:

"The kids were already questioning themselves as to what caused little Lil's death. For the police to question them so severely, added even more questions for them to ask themselves."

Not only do the parents have tremendous self-reproach, anger and anxiety, they also usually have intrusive thoughts, sometimes called frozen frames. We all have these and for the parents of SIDS babies, these thoughts usually pertain to the moments surrounding the time when they first found their child or heard the news, and the last time they were with the living child. *Did I do something wrong? Was he/she ill and I didn't recognize the symptoms? Did I place the child down wrong so he/she smothered?*
While we all tend to have sleep problems, parents of infants have a particularly difficult time, as they often wake up, believing they hear the cry of their baby.

Tanya:

"Just last week, Racheal said she woke up, thinking she heard Little Lil cry."

Caring for a baby during its first years of life is so time consuming that there is little time for anything else. The endless tasks of feeding, changing, and doctor appointments fill the parents' days. Then, when the baby suddenly dies, the parents feel a tremendous void in their lives, not only for their beloved child, but also for all the spaces of time that the child had filled. At first, they likely find themselves thinking Oh, my God! I need to check on _____." Then comes the sickening realization that their beloved child is dead. All the empty spaces in the parents' lives now produce "triggers," or intense grief reactions, not always by what happens, but also by what they're used to doing for their child that they no longer do.

Parents may be short-tempered with their other children and have difficulty talking or interacting with them. However, the usual response is just the opposite – they're over-protective. They may constantly check on their children when they're sleeping to be sure they are breathing, like the following father whose son, Craig, died from SIDS.

Father:

"I'm an early riser and the first thing I did **every morning** after Craig's death was go check to be sure my other children were breathing. After my last son, Josh, was born, I hardly slept until after he had lived past the age that Craig had died."

Parents sometimes report feeling the presence of loved ones that have gone on before the death of their child or grandchild.

Tanya:

"When I arrived at the hospital, I was totally frantic, irrational, - thought I was going crazy, but when I walked through the doors to the ER and saw Racheal   standing there, so forlorn, I think I felt little Lillie's namesake, her great grandmother, Lillie, touch me on the shoulder and say, 'Okay,

Tanya. I'm not there, so you have to be the strong one.' From that point on, I was strong and could be there for our children."

Footnote: Darin and Racheal had another baby – a little baby boy named Gabriel. However, Tanya said that Darin could never seem to shake the guilt, and he killed himself on the day before his birthday one year after Little Lil's death.

I definitely believe that police need better training in distinguishing between SIDS and abuse, and in showing sympathy and support to the distraught parents. In fact, they need to be more sympathetic of all people in grief.

After my husband's suicide, even though I had been with his daughter and her husband as we desperately searched for my husband, we were later separated and questioned. That was okay, but because I was functioning, getting coffee for people and talking, (I recognized from Joe's death that I was in shock and was thankful for it), one policeman said "I don't think you even care that your husband killed himself." There was almost an assault on a police officer that day…but I chose to walk away.

The following poem was written for Zac, Darin's brother, by Wanda Rose Wooley.

For Little Lil
Daddy, please don't look so sad.
Mommy, please don't cry,
Because I'm in the arms of Jesus
and He sings me Lullabies.
You see, I'm a special child and
am needed up above.
I'm the special gift you gave him.
A product of your love.

I'll always be there with you,
so watch the sky at night.
Look for the brightest star and
know that's my halo's brilliant light.
You'll see me in the morning frost
that mists your window pane.
That's me in the morning showers,
I'll be dancing in the rain.

When you feel a gentle breeze
from a gentle wind that blows,
You'll know it's me, planting
a kiss upon your nose.

Wanda Rose Wooley

Chapter XV
Death Following a Long Term Illness

We may know but never really accept the fact that illness will someday kill our child. Miracles do happen, or maybe we will beat the odds. Harsh facts about their condition may be presented to us time after time, but we desperately cling to hope.

When the diagnosis is given, we grieve, but then we often become so frantically involved with doctor appointments and treatments that we have little time to think, much less grieve. Parents often become their child's chief advocate; doctors are selected, treatments analyzed, choices made, and we wonder with every decision, *Is this the right choice?* Later, we question: *Would things have been different if ...?*

Mother:
> "We had to be so trusting of doctors, medical staff and hospitals. Were we getting the best advice possible? We were never sure."

Then, if the child goes into remission, life *almost* becomes normal again. Unfortunately, the dreaded disease rears its ugly head one more time, and the parents again face the terrifying fact that their child might die.

The greatest pain for the parents initially is seeing their child's suffering. They see such strength, such quiet determination, and many children (and adults) carry on a valiant battle to the end.

Mother:

"No one – and I mean NO one could have fought harder to live than my daughter. Her pain was prolonged beyond human endurance because of her extra-ordinary will to live. To have watched your daughter fight like that – and lose – makes me wonder; why fight anymore?

On a more peaceful note: *because* of watching my daughter's exceptional abilities in fighting her battles, and seeing her survive time after time in spite of one negative medical prognosis after another – I learned – and truly believe – that whatever is going to happen in this world will happen. If my daughter couldn't change her destiny – no one can. And this makes me a little 'easier' on myself and the vast amount of uncontrollable circumstances around us."

Most caregivers question the decisions they made, whether the patient was a child, spouse or parent. For example, my friend Judy lost her husband to cancer when he was a relatively young man.

Judy:

"Stanley made his own decisions concerning his treatments from the very beginning of his fight with colon cancer. He never admitted to having pain, but towards the end, he fidgeted and changed positions all the time, which suggested to me that he really did hurt. His doctor recommended morphine patches which I thought would make Stanley more comfortable. I talked him into it, and four days, two patches later, Stanley died. Now I feel guilty. Did I hasten his death?"

When my own mother was suffering from lung cancer (never smoked or was around smoke in her life), she pleaded, "Betty, please do not let them run more tests on me. They're so painful. It's okay – I'm ready to go." But I could not do that. I wanted her to live and maybe **this** *doctor would know what to do.* Now, this is one of my regrets; why did I cause my mother additional suffering by allowing more painful tests?

The *if onlys* are particularly difficult for parents whose child died from a serious illness. *Why didn't I listen when he complained? If only I had taken her to a doctor sooner, a different doctor, different hospital, different city, had more tests run...* The list goes on. We have to remember that we did our best with the limited knowledge that we had *at that time.* It is easy to see in hindsight how we might have handled things differently.

Chapter XVI
Sudden Death

"You can perhaps think it is a little thing, but to permit
someone to die, without a farewell, a single word
of comfort or understanding is a terrible thing to bear."

Meryl Streep in *Sophie's Choice*

If only we could have had one moment, just one last moment, to say I love you. But we did not, did we? Whether it was the crash of metal, the blast of a gun, or a last, single whisper of breath that ended our child's life, our lives changed forever.

We think of many different scenarios that might have changed that moment in time, and we re-play those scenarios, trying to change the outcome, but it does not change. Had our son or daughter left a few seconds earlier or later, they would not have met the killer car on an ice-covered bridge. Or, perhaps one fraction of an inch made the difference between life and death. Chance plays a much larger role in our lives than we ever realized before.

Mother: Cause of death of 17-year-old daughter:
> "Hit by piece of flying metal which severed carotid artery and jugular vein. Death was almost instant. Where? Local fair."

Different types of deaths cause variations in grief symptoms. Parents whose child died suddenly are more apt to have delayed or avoided grief. The shock renders us almost helpless. Denial tends to last longer. Parents of children that died from long-term illness have time to slowly absorb the facts, whereas in sudden death, the facts were thrown at us all at once. This doesn't mean that one type of death causes more pain than another; it's just different.

If your child died from risk-taking behavior, the *Teenager and Young Adult* section in the Suicide chapter of this book will likely help you.

I'm making it sound as if sudden deaths are the worst, but there are trade-offs. Would we rather see our child suffer in agonizing pain for months, maybe years if they have an incurable disease, hooked up to IVs, experience hope, only to have it dashed time after time? See the questions in their hurting, innocent eyes, *Can't you make the pain go away, Daddy?* Or, if older, *Why me, Lord, why me?* Would we rather have had a miscarriage and not have memories? There is simply no good way or good time for a child to die.

Chapter XVII
Suicide

Something I didn't tell you in "Our Story" (Chapter I)

My husband, Gene, had gone to a treatment center for alcohol addiction two months before Joe's death; then, after one slip, he remained *clean and sober* for seven years. He was Joe's stepfather, but he loved Joe. I told him during this time that he was the *Wind Beneath my Wings*.

However, one afternoon, he went to a neighbor's house to help with a plumbing problem. When he started to leave, the neighbor and visiting friends offered him a beer, which he declined. Unfortunately, on the way to his truck, he passed by one of their pickups and in the back was a tub filled with iced-down beer. That could be the end of the story, because it was the beginning of the end. He reached in and got one.

There's a saying in Alcoholics Anonymous: "One drink is too many; a thousand isn't enough." That one drink led to another, and another... Gene wanted so badly to quit drinking, but he seemed haunted by demons that I did not understand. Treatment center after treatment center, and he still drank. Alcohol was ruining his business, his relationships with family, and certainly, his self-esteem. He fought the battle for a long time, but the power of alcohol finally won. One beautiful October morning, about five years after that iced-down beer, Gene committed suicide. He "swallowed a bullet," as I had heard him say of others. He put a .38 pistol in his mouth and pulled the trigger.

Even though there had been other close calls, I never believed he would take his own life. He seemed to be such a strong person, except in this one area. He apparently preferred death to the addiction he could not *kick*.

After Joe's death, I had thought "I've been through the worse thing possible, I can survive anything," and, I still think that. However, with Gene's death, I not only grieved his death, but I again grieved for Joe. My grief symptoms were totally different than my grief symptoms had been after Joe's death. With Joe, I had felt guilt and overwhelming pain, sadness, and hopelessness. With Gene, I felt **ANGER!** The paramedic, a friend of mine, later said that I was radiating with anger, and I really don't know why. I remember telling one friend who came as soon as she heard to go home. The policeman asking me questions said something I did not like, and I turned on my heels and left him talking to the air. He could get those answers another day as far as I was concerned. That was totally unlike me, but my anger and anxiety did not dissipate for months.

I also felt tremendous anxiety, and my only relief was walking. My sister-in-law would call and ask if I needed to walk, and I would always say "Yes." We walked for hours every day. In addition, I developed a sudden fear of high bridges, which I talk about in the chapter on *Fear*. I still do not try the really high upper levels, but that's okay.

Gene was a wonderful man, but the power of addiction took his life, and consequently, changed mine forever.

Suicide

I don't know why...
I'll never know why...
I don't have to know why...
I don't like it...

115

I don't have to like it...

What I do have to do is make a choice
about my living.
What I do want to do is accept it and
go on living.
The choice is mine.

I can go on living, valuing every moment
in a way I never did before,
Or I can be destroyed by it and, in turn, destroy others.
I thought I was immortal, that my children
and my family were also,
That tragedy happened only to others...
But I know now that life is tenuous and valuable.

And I choose to go on living,
Making the most of the time I have.
And valuing my family and friends
In a way I never experienced before.
...Iris Bolton
Author of *MY SON, MY SON*

Suicide is so difficult to accept and understand because it seems so preventable. The *if onlys* and *should haves* play havoc with our emotions when our loved one takes his or her own life.

Teenagers and Young Adults:
So often with teenagers and young adults, the reason for the suicide seems so trivial... perhaps he had just broken up with his girlfriend, or it was the end result of an argument. On a personal note, how could my son, Joe, make the decision to lie down in

the middle of the road, regardless of how rejected or depressed he felt? While doing research for this chapter, I read something that helped me better understand impulsive teen behavior.

While our teenagers or young adults may think they are quite adult, capable of making great decisions, their brain simply has not reached maturity yet. Part of the brain is mature – the part where *impulses to act originate.* However, the part that *controls those impulses* and *balances risk and reward* does not mature until the mid 20s, and this is the part of the brain that determines how much priority is given to messages like *Do it now*, versus *What are the consequences?* [1 (63-70); 2 (113-120)]

> "The teenage brain is like a car
> with a good accelerator but a weak brake." [3] *
> Laurence Steinberg
> Temple University
> Psychology Professor and Researcher

The parts of the brain that arouse a teen emotionally and make him pay attention to peer pressure and the rewards of action – the gas pedal – are probably all set. But the brakes, the part that helps a teen consider the consequences of those actions, resist sudden impulses and peer pressure, are still developing. Parents may be baffled when their teen can make an A+ on an algebra exam (part of the brain thats basically mature by age 16), yet impulsively do dumb things and take stupid risks (part of the brain that does not mature until mid-20s). We wonder, *What were they thinking!* [3 (116)] *

Teens typically have feelings of being invincible and immortal. While they are capable of knowing right from wrong and making rational decisions, they're more likely than adults to act impulsively without fully considering the consequences, especially when confronted with an emotional or stressful decision.*

Why this lapse in brain maturity? Poor design? Actually, it serves a very valuable purpose, though it may have proven to be a disastrous time for our child. This time of *elasticity* in the brain helps the adolescent or young adult adapt to his environment, whether it was to yesterdays' ice-age, or today's fast-paced, high-tech world.

Almost as soon as our child reaches the terrible teens, Mom and Dad just aren't very smart anymore. Had he or she lived, we would have eventually become friends - and smart - again. It is particularly difficult for parents if there was an argument before the act, or if the parents were attempting to practice *tough love*. We are never given the chance to *make it right* again.

Father of Karen:

"Our 22-year-old daughter had attempted suicide with a razor, and we were rushing her to the hospital when she suddenly bailed out of the car. Slamming on my brakes, I frantically jumped out and ran towards her, praying that 'my baby' was still alive. However, just as I was about to reach her, she sprang up and ran from me. When I finally caught her, **I was furious**. I said terrible things to her. She had put not only her life in danger, but other peoples' lives in danger too. Those words that I *yelled* at her have been part of the guilt I've experienced. Now, it's too late."

Mother of Karen:

"After we had entered our daughter into the

hospital for attempting suicide with a razor, I told my husband, 'Next time, she'll be sure she does it right.' And she did. One month later, she used a gun to end her own life."

We have a tendency, as parents, to think that we are somehow to blame. Whether it's true or not, we believe that others are questioning and condemning our parenting skills. And we do too. *What did I do wrong?* We lash ourselves with mental whips. We may know that our guilt is irrational but still have to struggle with it time after time.

Because Joe's death was so questionable, I, at first, felt it was a self-destructive act; he was depressed and did not care if he lived or died, and that must be my fault! I was giving Joe no responsibility for his actions. I will never forget one of my nephews pointing out to me, "Aunt Betty! Joe went to a Labor Day party. You didn't force him to go. **He** chose to drink. You didn't pour beer down his throat! Quit taking all the blame for **his** actions." I will love you forever, Kerry, for saying that. It helped.

When our child takes his own life, anger often plays a major role in our grief process. We are angry at our child for giving up a beautiful, promising life and for causing us a life of pain without them. Were we not going to raise a loving, happy family with doting grandchildren? Our child took those dreams from us, and we are angry. Plus, we are angry for all the usual reasons bereaved parents are angry.

Because Iris Bolton, unknowingly, was so much comfort to me, I would like to quote from an article she wrote in a Compassionate Friends newsletter.[5]

"....I have suggested that we, as parents, can only guide, advise, suggest, inform, persuade. We can only offer ourselves, our humanness – our best selves and sometimes our worst selves. What our child does with that is **his** responsibility and his alone. We cannot insure that our child will have our values, morals or goals. Ultimately, it is the child's decision regarding what he does with what we offer him. He was responsible for his life and I am responsible for my life. I must stay aware of that fact."

This is about the time in a teen's world when his friends become his beacon of light, and he or she may experiment with alcohol and/or drugs to fit in with the crowd. Since chemicals typically lessen inhibitions and self-doubts, the teen then *feels* that he now belongs. Unfortunately, chemicals also increase the likelihood that self-destructive impulses will become actual behavior.

We mistakenly often believe that it is the peer pressure of the *moment*, "Just say 'No,'" that causes a teenager pain, but in actuality, it is often the feelings afterward of being excluded by his friends. After the teen says *No*, as instructed, he is no longer a part of the group. They band together to discuss the *fun* they had, and he is alone. Unfortunately, this feeling of being alone carries an easy solution – go along with the crowd.

To be excluded or even worse, to be ridiculed by so-called *friends*, is totally devastating. For someone to feel rejected by friends, alienated from those he/she admires is one factor found to predict who will most likely commit suicide. The Interpersonal Theory of Suicide calls it "failed belongingness." [6 (pp.6-14)] This, plus the teen's tendency to be impulsive and to not consider consequences, are likely two reasons for high substance abuse and suicide in teens.

Chemical Dependency: (For more on this subject, see chapter on **Drug Overdose**)

When our loved one moves from chemical use to abuse to dependency, he or she often has feelings of hopelessness and despair. He or she might "quit" time after time, to no avail. My husband Gene would swear on the Bible, his mother's grave, on Joe's grave, to me and to our minister that he was going to quit. He would think up rituals. One time he rounded up all the stashed liquor bottles and asked me to go to the dump that is on our place with him. He placed each bottle carefully upon a berm and systematically called to each before blasting it with a gun: "I'm through with you, you S.O.B. You no longer control my life." or "You no longer have power over me…" Nothing worked. He tried everything but could not quit. I think his suicide was an act of desperation from feeling so powerless due to his addiction.

> No conflict is so severe as his who labours
> To subdue himself.
> Thomas Kemps (1380 – 1471)
> *Imitation of Christ*

Individuals often become addicted to pain medication after accidents, surgeries, and other pain causing conditions. Again, the helpless feeling of not being able to quit the medication arises, and feelings of hopelessness often give rise to feelings of worthlessness.

Amy's Story: (Not a bereaved parent, but the shock and devastation are quite similar.)

I fell in love with Alvin almost as soon as I met him. He was the most amazing, awesome man I had ever met. We were together for seven years;

six of which were beautiful; the last was living Hell.

What happened? Alvin worked in the oil fields, a very dangerous line of work. One day, a piece of casing fell on his head, hitting his hard hat, then glancing off and breaking both his shoulder and arm. Had the casing hit him in the middle of the head, with or without hard hat, it would have killed him.

Alvin was a hearty, healthy man and probably had known little pain in his life. Or, maybe he had an addictive personality or a genetic tendency towards addiction. I don't know. At any rate, he ate the pain pills like candy. After about three weeks, the doctor refused to refill his prescription. On the way to work one day, he asked his co-workers, "Does anyone have anything strong for pain?" One guy answered, "Not anything legal, but I have something that will really help." It turned out to be crack cocaine.

Alvin evolved from smoking crack to shooting-up "ice," then using almost any and everything he could find. I knew little of what was going on at this time because I had always loved and trusted him. However, one day he said we needed to talk. I was horrified to learn that we were $50,000.00 in debt; he had borrowed everywhere, then maxed out our credit cards. He explained that the debts were due to his drug use, but he was going to quit. He knew he could with my help.

However, it wasn't long before he was sneaking around, I was missing money, and he was staying out "trippin". Because I wouldn't give him money, he introduced my fourteen-year-old daughter to drugs, telling her he would share them with her if she would get money from me.

He alternated between having violent, paranoid rages and being apologetic. I became very frightened of him. When apologetic, he would make statements like, "You'd be better off without me," or, "Someday I won't be here in your way."

One day he came in and started riffling through every drawer, every shelf, every cabinet. I asked, "What in the world are you looking for?"

He replied, "I've lost something important." Unbeknownst to me, he was actually rounding up all the pills he could find - of any kind. I was taking high blood pressure and anxiety medication, so he took those pills, plus antibiotics, aspirin – everything he could find - plus all the drugs he had "stashed."

We thought he was asleep on the living room floor until I found the empty pill bottles. We called 911, he was rushed to the hospital, his stomach pumped and he was given charcoal to absorb the drugs. I begged the doctor to help or get help for Alvin. But the doctor was hardly civil to us. Alvin had poured on the charm and told the doctor, "I just took a few pills so I could get some sleep. They [my mother and I] just want to have me committed so Amy can have my insurance money." Alvin had no insurance; he had been fired two weeks before this incident. At any rate, the doctor refused to help, other than to get the drugs out of his system.

I told the male nurse that Alvin would probably try to escape, but he assured us that no one could get past him. Alvin did. We found him wandering the streets, shoeless.

The next nine days were filled with out-of-control rages and paranoid accusations, usually followed by apologies. On the evening of the ninth day, he apologized and told me to go on to bed and he would be there soon.

The next morning, I got up, put on the coffee and called to Alvin that coffee was almost ready. But I couldn't find him. I called and looked through the house, but no Alvin. Then I checked the garage. I could see through the vehicles that he was sitting down, but something was terribly wrong. As I got closer, I saw that he had hanged himself with a bungee cord. I went into total shock and hysterics. It was unbelievable to me that the man I loved could end up this way. It had taken one year for Alvin to change from the man I loved to someone almost alien to me. I had been naive because I so wanted things to be like they once were. I never gave up hope, but apparently, Alvin did.

The addictive qualities of today's drugs take their toll and often turn our loved one into someone we do not know. Many teens and young adults may believe that "club drugs" are benign, but they usually are not. For example, some drugs, such as cocaine and methamphetamine, can seriously affect the neurotransmitters in the brain and the damage may be long-lasting, even permanent. Although the drugs probably cause the individual to *feel good* for the moment, he or she may be unable to feel good *naturally* for a very long time. Lasting consequences may result.

A strong connection exists between substance abuse, mental disorders (including depression) and self-harm. Which comes first? Does the depressed person attempt to self medicate, or does the substance abuser become depressed? Research indicates that some forty percent of alcoholics have episodes of major depression and in two/thirds of these cases, depression appears to be secondary to alcohol abuse. [7 (p. 23)] In a review of risk factors for adolescent suicide and suicidal behavior, researchers have found that mental disorders, including depression and chemical use, are the most important. Each is more of a risk if combined with the other. [8 (pp. 52-63)]

One *mother* in the survey whose son had apparently died in an alcohol related accident, described her emotions as follows:

> [I feel....]
> *"Regret* that his life wasn't less *tortured*, as he called it (since his Dad died of suicide after a "fuss" with this same sixteen-year-old.)
> *Guilt* that I couldn't *fix* his drinking addiction.
> *Anger* that he didn't have the strength or inspiration to fix his life!
> *Anger* at a world with these addictive options.
> *Fear* that it could happen to another of my three remaining children (all daughters)."

Chronic depression likely runs in her family, as she also stated: "have been too closely associated with too many depressed persons – father, first husband (deceased), son (deceased), and two of my three remaining children." A genetic chemical imbalance is usually involved when depression runs through the generations. This family did seek help, and the son was in rehab twice, but sometimes no matter what we do, it isn't enough. We can even see it coming but can still do nothing. That may be difficult for someone who hasn't been there to believe, but it's definitely possible, especially where severe depression, drugs and/or alcohol or mental illness is concerned.

Chronic Depression and other Mental Illness:
Because suicide is so often the end result of chronic depression and/or mental illness, it is sometimes argued that suicide is not a choice. Part of the definition of the word, *choice*, suggests that we have the opportunity or privilege to choose freely. But does the pre-suicidal individual really have that freedom? Some believe not. The person that takes his own life likely feels that he's at the *end of his rope* and simply wants to end the pain.

> "There is no suffering greater than that which drives people to suicide; suicide defines the moment in which mental pain exceeds the human capacity to bear it. It represents the abandonment of hope."
>
> ...John T. Maltsberger, M.D.
> Practicing psychiatrist and past president of
> the American Association of Suicidology.

Anti-depressants often help, but many times they do not. Much research is being done on the relationship between depression and chemical imbalances in the brain, and while anti-depressants are generally designed to increase levels of certain neurotransmitters, known as *messengers of the brain*, they only work about 65% of the time. It is still a very inexact science. Unfortunately, even if an anti-depressant IS going to work, it takes considerable time to "kick in", and a suicidal person is very vulnerable during this time. Sadly, it may not work at all. [9] While the majority of depressed people are not suicidal, 60% of those who die by suicide suffer from major depression. If one includes alcoholics who are depressed, this figure rises to over 75%. [10]

We, as parents, often do not distinguish depression from typical teen or young-adult moodiness. We know less of what is going on in their minds due to their normal gravitation towards peers and withdrawal from parents. But, after our child's suicide, we think we *should* have known. With older children, he or she may have simply deceived us so we wouldn't worry, or we did not live close enough to recognize the symptoms of depression.

Norman Vincent Peale quoted parts of a very poignant memorial service for a young man who had died by his own hand. The service was conducted by the young man's pastor, the Rev. Weston Stevens, who eloquently described a suicidal person's battle between life and death. I think its very good and had it read at my husbands funeral.

When Someone Takes His Own Life

"Our friend died on his own battlefield. He was killed in action fighting a civil war. He fought against adversaries that were as real to him as his casket is real to us. They were powerful adversaries. They took toll of his energies and endurance. They exhausted the last vestiges of his courage and strength. At last these adversaries overwhelmed him. And it appeared that he lost the war. But did he? I see a host of victories that he has won!

For one thing–he has won our admiration- -because even if he lost the war, we give him credit for his bravery on the battlefield. And we give

127

him credit for the courage and pride and hope that he used as his weapons as long as he could. We shall remember not his death, but his daily victories gained through his kindnesses, and thoughtfulness, through his love for family and friends, for animals and books and music, for all things beautiful, lovely and honorable. We shall remember not his last day of defeat, but we shall remember the many days that he was victorious over overwhelming odds. We shall remember not the years we thought he had left, but the intensity with which he lived the years he had!

Only God knows what this child of his suffered in the silent skirmishes that took place in his soul. But our consolation is that God does know, and understands." [11] (p.35)

Schizophrenia:

Three mothers in the survey had children with schizophrenia who died by suicide, but likely all mothers and fathers of children who suffered with this disease will agree with the mother who said "I miss my child – but not the illness." So often, the parents had suffered considerably with the child *prior* to his suicide. Hope likely gave way to despair, back to hope, back to despair – a roller-coaster of frustration, hope, pain, sorrow.

Apparently the medication for schizophrenia causes the person taking it to feel miserable and lifeless; consequently, the tendency is to quit taking it. When I was getting my Masters Degree, one of my professors told about having a prescription incorrectly filled at the pharmacy. The medication was for schizophrenia - not for his illness. He said one pill made him an absolute zombie for two days. After feeling totally worthless and unable to function for those two days and realizing what the medication was actually for, he said he better understood the schizophrenic's reluctance to take his meds.

One mother I know told about her son, Chris, who did not want to take his medication: "Mom, all I do is sleep when I take it. I feel awful. I'm OK now and don't need it anymore." It's difficult to force a young adult to take his medication. During one of his *episodes*, my friend, Sheri, called a psychiatrist and begged him to see her son. He said he had to talk with her son.

When Chris was asked if he was taking his medication and he replied, "No," the psychiatrist refused to see him. One week later, Chris used a high powered rifle to end his own life.

Another mother, whose twenty-year-old son died by suicide, wrote the following:

"Early in the episode of schizophrenia, (fifteen years of trouble), the doctors blamed us, the two parents! We refused to accept [blame]. The law gave us trouble when our son was episodic. At dismissal from the hospital, I would be given a phone number to call when my son needed help. Each time, I would be told to call other numbers. Then, about the fourth or fifth person would tell me to call the original number. The old run around!"

Not only does the schizophrenic likely feel *different*, that he does not belong, but he may also feel like he is a total burden to his family and friends. One of three factors found to predict suicidality is *perceived burdensomeness*; the individual feels that he/she is a burden to family, friends and possibly society as a whole. (The other two are *failed belongingness*, discussed in the peer pressure segment of Teens and Young Adults [in this chapter], and *acquired capability*, simply meaning that the individual, by getting used to pain and fear from previous attempts, has decreased fear of pain and self-injury in the future. He or she is more likely to try again, unfortunately, with greater success.) [7] (p.33)

However, schizophrenics are less likely than those with other diagnoses to have engaged in self-harm activities prior to committing suicide, so there is less warning. They are also more likely to use more frightening methods to end their lives. [7] (p. 42) One mother, when asked where and how her child died, wrote, "behind a filling station by self-immolation."

Schizophrenia is a sad illness and too little is known about its treatment. The medications apparently keep the individual from experiencing the horrible symptoms of schizophrenia, but they also have tremendous side effects. The natural tendency is for the person to quit taking them, sometimes with disastrous results.

Bipolar Disorder:

Bipolar Disorder is characterized by both depressive episodes and episodes of elevated and/or irritable mood. While the depressive episodes are less lengthy and severe than in major depression, bipolar disorder is also quite lethal. Studies of bipolar patients indicate that twenty-five to fifty percent of persons with this illness make at least one suicide attempt during their lifetime, and an estimated three to twenty percent die by suicide. [10] (pp. 1-2)

Dysthymic Disorder:

This disorder is characterized by symptoms of depression of lower severity than those of major depression._[7] (pp. 31-32)

Eating disorders:

While both bulimia nervosa (BN) and anorexia nervosa (AN) have increased suicidal ideation and suicide attempts, AN alone

130

confers risk by suicide. Anorexia nervosa is one of the deadliest of all mental illnesses. Those who suffer from it are more likely to die from suicide than malnutrition. [7 (p. 36)]

Borderline Personality Disorder:
Borderline Personality Disorder manifests itself through impulsivity, poor self-esteem, intense mood swings, storminess in personal relationships, and nonsuicidal self-injury. [7 (pp. 43-47)]

All of the above disorders increase risk of suicide to some extent; the risk being considerably more than that of the general population. The parent may have felt they were dealing with a time bomb, hoping against hope, that it wouldn't go off. Or, their child's suicide may have been a total surprise.

The conditions discussed in this chapter, immaturity of youth, chemical abuse or dependency, and depression and/or other mental disorders usually do not stand alone. They are often interrelated. For example, the immature youth abuses alcohol to fit in, the person with a mood disorder likely self-medicates with alcohol or drugs, and the chemically dependent person becomes depressed because his life is out of control.

Simply a thought: Most people do not understand:
While writing this chapter, I was discussing suicide with a friend, and he simply could not understand how anything can be so tragic or terrible that there's no way past it besides taking your own life. And it is difficult for those of us not struggling with any of the above conditions to understand. We do know days of happiness and/or we do have hopes of being happy again. We've come through hard times and we know we can get through this one too. The suicidal person has given up hope. He or she may have tried again and again to give up chemicals and suffered failure after

failure. The depressed person likely felt that the pain of living was worse than the thought of dying. Those suffering from mood disorders probably struggled with their loss of control over their disease. When will the next episode engulf them, rendering them helpless to live a normal life and causing them to be a burden to others? While we perceive them as having had a choice, they likely felt that they had none.

How do we, as parents, survive the suicide of our child? Since we tend to have tremendous self-blame, we have to let the responsibility of our child's actions be on our child.

His or her actions were not our choice. The decisions we made concerning our child were in our child's best interest, or so we thought at the time. We have to forgive ourselves and others – and our child.

Chapter XVIII
Homicide

Four sad but powerful stories will be told in this chapter. Each story is told by someone, like you, whose life has been forever altered by a deliberate, violent act of another. To make matters worse, the person who murdered or caused the death of your loved one had a choice; your loved one had none.

I cannot thank the four individuals (Steve, Jo Ann, Kim and Jim) enough who shared their stories and inner thoughts with me. Our hopes are that their stories will help you in some way. Each of them said: "If there's even a chance my story will help another person affected by homicide, then please tell my story." A special thanks goes to Jo Ann Starkey, Dallas Contact Person for Parents Of Murdered Children, Inc. for making this chapter possible. Her story is one of the four.

The unique and different dimensions of homicide grief will be woven in with these stories.

Steve's Story:

Kelsey, my eleven-year-old daughter, was excited to be entering the sixth grade, and of course, she needed new clothes for this big event. It was tax-free weekend, so what better time to buy new outfits! She and her mother, my ex-wife Evelyn*, struck off for the mall on Thursday to make selections and planned to return the following day to

* Evelyn: Assumed name

purchase their *finds* when *tax-free* would actually apply.

As part of our divorce settlement, Evelyn and I had recently agreed to joint custody; Kelsey would alternate weeks with her mother and me. I was due to pick Kelsey up at her mother's home at 6:00 pm every other Friday, and since this particular Friday preceded the beginning of the school year, I had been thinking of special things we could do during our week together. Perhaps go fishing or attend a baseball game over the weekend? Meet her mother at a restaurant for dinner to give a show of solidarity? What would Kelsey like best?

Steve and daughter, Kelsey

Kelsey enjoying life

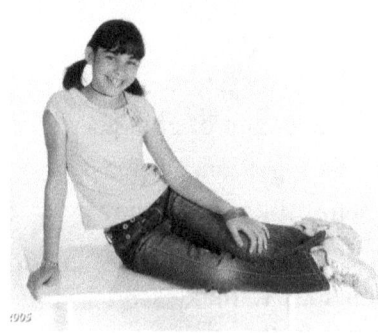

Kelsey

134

Early Friday morning, Evelyn called to say that Kelsey was complaining of an upset stomach and would not be going to gymnastics daycare that day. She asked if I planned to attend *Meet the Teacher Night* that evening and I told her, "No, I'll just pick Kelsey up at your house at 6:00 pm as planned."

Kelsey and her mother ended up going back to the mall later that morning to pick up the clothing they had selected the day before. After shopping and having lunch, they returned home.

I was still at work around 4:00 pm when I received a call. However, when I answered, the caller hung up. Probably a wrong number or a telephone solicitor's call.

When I arrived at Evelyn's house shortly after 6:00 pm to pick up Kelsey, I knocked – but no one came to the door. I called Evelyn's cell phone, but it went straight to voice mail. "Strange," I thought, "since they're expecting me." I then called a mutual friend, Susan,* to see if she knew where they might be, but she did not. However, she revealed that she had a key to Evelyn's house and insisted on coming right over. When she arrived, she instructed me to remain in the car while she went inside, so I did, but I kept thinking, *something's not right*. In a short while, Susan rushed out of the house looking totally ashen, so I jumped out of my car to see what was wrong. She told me to call 911; however, when the operator asked the purpose of the call, I had to say, "I don't know! I

* Susan: assumed name

135

was told to call you, but I don't know why. I am giving the phone to the person who told me to call you." As I handed the phone to Susan, I rushed towards the front porch and entered the house. "Kelsey? Kelsey!" I first checked the living areas, then headed for her bedroom, still calling her name. Then I saw her. Kelsey was lying on the floor, face up, with her eyes closed as if asleep. But she didn't answer when I called her name. My mind was racing. What happened? Kelsey was totally unresponsive.

Susan then called from the outside doorway, "Steve! Come outside now! The 911 operator said we must leave the house immediately."

But, I didn't. "Something's wrong, Susan! I need to give Kelsey CPR."

"NO!" She started back into the house, yelling for me to come outside. "Get out of the house NOW and wait for the first responders to arrive."

I finally headed outside while calling Evelyn's name. Perhaps she knew what was going on, but she didn't answer either.

The first responders seemed to take forever to arrive, and I was startled to find out later that it had only taken about three minutes. The mind does play tricks on us.

After several minutes, Evelyn was brought out on a gurney – but where was Kelsey? I asked the EMT responders about Kelsey's condition and when another ambulance would arrive for her, but no one would give me any answers. I felt so distraught and frustrated. By this time, I knew something terrible had happened, but I didn't know exactly what.

When the Chaplain of the police department finally arrived, he conferred with the other officers, then came to me. With sorrow in his voice, he said, "Mr. Roberts, there is no easy way for me to tell you this, but your daughter is dead." Total shock, bewilderment and *pain* enveloped me. I did not know it at the time, but it's protocol for the police that only the Chaplain can give official notification of a person's death. And that's what he did on Friday, August 5, 2005, the day my life changed forever. Kelsey, my baby and only child, was dead.

I called my parents, who hurriedly made arrangements to leave their home the following morning and drive the seven hours to my home. We made funeral arrangements for Kelsey over the weekend, but I desperately needed to know what had happened. On Monday afternoon, I went to the police station and met with the lieutenant and some of the officers who were at my ex-wife's home on August 5. I could hardly believe what I learned there. My ex-wife, Kelsey's own mother, had killed our daughter. She had apparently slipped an Ambien (hypnotic sleep medication) into Kelsey's food while they were at the mall, then smothered her with a bed sheet when they returned home. Detectives said that Kelsey had apparently desperately fought for her life. The Medical Examiner's office determined Kelsey's time of death between 12:00 noon and 2:30 pm.

Evelyn had also attempted to take her own life. Detectives of the police department found two places in the house where she had attempted, unsuccessfully, to hang herself. She had ended up cutting her left wrist and consuming a large quantity of Ambien. The first responders found her in her bed asleep and loudly snoring.

I later determined from phone records that the 4:00 pm telephone call I had received when I was at work had been made by Evelyn. After her call to my office, she also called the National Poison Control Hotline and a nearby pharmacy.

So many questions, but, no answers. Earlier that year when Evelyn learned of my intention to file for a divorce, she asserted, "Steve, I will grant you a divorce, but you're not taking Kelsey." I had thought she was just being dramatic, and we would work out the custody issues. That was not to be.

Either before or after killing Kelsey, Evelyn had carved a suicide note into the top of the cherry wood dining room table. Following is the message she wrote:

"I cannot live with the pain you've caused me and Kelsey. Now, she'll always be happy and in one place. She cries and prays every night that she will have her family back. She won't ever have to go back and forth again. I'd rather go to Hell than live without you and our family."

I had never heard Kelsey cry or complain when she stayed with me. She appeared to be taking our divorce quite well.

Evelyn had also used a knife to slash the seat cushions on the dining room chairs, as well as all of the cushions on the sofa and chairs in the living room. Furniture in every room of her home had been damaged or destroyed by knife marks and scrapings before she had attempted to kill herself.

After Evelyn regained consciousness in the hospital where she had been transported, she was taken to the county jail where she remained incarcerated until her trial. Although she pled not guilty by reason of insanity, the jury found her guilty and sentenced her to 80 years in prison. She will be eligible for parole after having served 30 years. Evelyn will be 80 years old when her first parole hearing is scheduled.

After Kelsey's death, I wondered, "How do I go on living?"

I'll Always Be Your Dad
Song by Alan Pedersen

Years have come and gone and time has surely drifted by.
I've searched for any answer, yet I'm left to wonder why.
One thing that I know for sure through the happy and the sad,
No matter what the circumstance, I will always be your dad.

Not a day goes by that I don't hold you in my heart;
My love reaches far beyond this space we are apart.
These empty arms remember all the good times that we had.
I may be standing here alone, but I will always be your dad.

Some don't understand so I won't bother to explain.
They look into my eyes but they can only see the pain,

Afraid to look too deep as they are blinded by the fear.
If only they could know a father's love can't disappear.

So when this road gets lonely and the journey seems too hard
And I start feeling sorry that I didn't get a card,
I just close my eyes and I can almost hear you say,
I love you and I miss you daddy...Happy Fathers Day.

One of the characteristics of parents whose child has been murdered is that they feel violated that someone has *chosen* to take their child's life. How could someone do that! It's inconceivable and leaves the parents feeling hurt, angry and vulnerable.

Steve:

"I cannot fathom how she [ex-wife] could give birth, love and care for Kelsey, then kill her own daughter. I just cannot understand."

Jo Ann:

"The very morning that my precious son, Brian, was murdered, I was sentenced to a life of pain and suffering because of one man's <u>choices</u> and actions – a man I had never met. I did not have the privilege of a trial and appeals. I was convicted and sentenced by a depraved young man with a .357 gun in his hand loaded with 'hollow point' bullets. When he chose to put that gun to my son's head and pull the trigger, he blew a hole in my son's head and a hole in my heart and soul – and a hole in the heart and soul of Brian's sister, Renee – that will never heal."

Kim sent me a song by Jewel that means much to her; now it does to me, too.

The Shape of You in <u>*The Shape of You*</u> album by Jewel:
>   (Chorus)
>   "There's a hole in my heart and I'll carry it wherever I go,
>   Like a treasure that travels with me down every road.
>   There's this longing, lonesome ending, kind of bitter, kind of sweet.
>   There's a hole in my heart in the shape of you."

Jo Ann's Story

A mother's love for her children is a special love that is given with her whole heart and one that is felt deep within her soul. Most of all, it creates a bond that is as unbreakable as it is eternal.

Brian had been a much-wanted and planned-for child, born almost fifteen months after the tragic premature stillborn deaths of twin sisters, Kelly and Shelly Higgins. When Brian was two and one-half, his father chose to leave, and his older sister, Renee, became his *second mommy*. Later, I remarried, and Brian gained a new step-dad (Duane) and three new siblings.

Brian was a real pleasure to his family (usually). He grew into a typical teenager, having many moods and wanting to be accepted by his friends. One day he came home and totally shocked me when he said, "Mom, I need a break from school. Scott, Lance and I are going to Florida and be beach

Jo Ann

Brian's last Christmas

Brians graduation picture

bums for awhile."

"WHAT? Brian! How are you going to do that?"

"It'll be OK, Mom. We'll get jobs and do just fine. We're just tired of school, Texas heat, and not having any beaches nearby. I'll come back and finish school. This isn't forever."

I tried to talk him out of it. "Brian, what if I forbid you to go?"

With a twinkle in his eye and a quirky smile, he said, "I'm going, Mom." And go he did. Little did I know that he would be safer there than home.

The three of them went to Florida, found jobs and led a carefree, seemingly happy life for about a year. Then, one day Brian called and asked: "Mom, we're coming home. Do I still have a bedroom there, or do I need to get my own apartment?" I told him we would love to have him home. Our home was his home. I was elated. Perhaps home, Texas heat, and school weren't so bad after all.

But school was not going to be in the equation that year. "Mom, you know I drive an old clunker. I want to work for a year and get a better car. Then I'll go back to school." I couldn't disagree that his car was an old clunker, so I reluctantly agreed. Also, he was still making up his mind about what he wanted to study - for him to go back to school now just might be a waste of his time and our money.

While in Florida, Brian had worked for a luxury resort hotel, a job that helped him quickly get hired by the Lowes Anatole Hotel in Dallas. He seemed to really like that line of work. In fact, when I mentioned to him the possibility of making Hotel Management his major, I saw a spark in his eyes that said "Hey! That isn't a bad idea!" Meanwhile, he would be getting good work experience while saving money for a car. Everything seemed to be working as planned until one ill-fated night.

On that night, Brian and several of his co-workers finished their midnight shift and went to Snookies Bar and Grill to eat. One of the girls in the group, Natonia, had been dating a security guard, Andrew Morrison, who also worked at the

Anatole. However, she broke her date with Andrew that night because she was worried about her friend, Eric, who was distraught because his girlfriend had suddenly ended their relationship that day. She asked Eric to go to Snookies with them instead of Andrew; unfortunately, Andrew also showed up at Snookies.

Andrew came into the bar and passed by the table where Brian's group was sitting. He spoke to no one but gave Natonia a scathing, dirty look. Although he appeared to be quite intoxicated, he headed straight for the bar and drank even more. Eventually, Natonia joined Andrew at the bar. They talked and quarreled, but in a little while, the two of them came back to Brian's table and sat down.

Brian's group was ready to leave, but Andrew said "NO! Don't go." He quickly ordered a round of *shots* for everyone to keep them there. When the bar and grill was ready to close, Andrew still wanted to party. "Y'all come to my room. We'll party there." No one wanted to go.

Natonia was afraid for Andrew to drive, so she confiscated his car keys and asked another of the group, Victor, to take him home, but Victor said, "No way. I'm not going to babysit your drunk boy-friend."

She then asked Brian, who would do anything to help a friend. I look back and think how that was both one of his good and his bad qualities. He wouldn't take the trash out for Mom without grumbling, but if a friend asked him to do something, by golly, he would do it in a minute.

Brian did take Andrew to his room, which turned out to be in a down-trodden, extended-stay motel. Brian apparently went in for a minute, sat down on the end corner of the bed and was facing the TV when Andrew came up from behind, put a gun point-blank to Brian's head and pulled the trigger. Detectives believe that Brian was totally unaware of the gun being placed to his head.

The very gun that Andrew used to supposedly protect lives at the Anatole, was used to kill a fine, innocent young man who was simply trying to do a favor for a friend. Brian was being a *Good Samaritan,* but Andrew killed him point-blank, then threw the gun in nearby bushes.

Supposedly, after being placed in jail, Andrew kept mumbling, "Eric," the name of the boy Natonia was attempting to help that night. In his extremely intoxicated mind, did Andrew think he was shooting Eric? Or was he jealous of Brian because Natonia had been flirting with him?

Morrison was later found to have skipped bond in California on an arrest for reckless driving, DWI, speeding, suspended driver's license, and for resisting arrest. He was a fugitive from California when he was hired by the hotel.

I received the call that changed my life forever at 6:15 am on May 23, 1994, from Parkland Hospital. I learned that my son, Brian, had been shot in the head and was on life support. We rushed to the hospital, but 30 minutes later, my precious Brian was dead. I was plunged into the blackest hell imaginable, followed by a pain so intense that even breathing became an unendurable labor.

Morrison was convicted of first-degree murder and sentenced to fifty-five years in prison, where he remains at this time.

In the meantime, our lives as we knew them to be on that fateful and devastating morning were shattered in a split second. I long to see Brian's handsome face and his unique smile and hear his sweet voice say, "Mom, I love you, too," and, "Mom, don't worry – I'll be all right! You worry too much!"

Brian, you will live forever in our hearts, and we will love you and miss you forever and always!

Brian, your smile warmed our hearts,
Your laughter brightened our days,
And your life, your love, and your death
Changed our lives forever.

(Submitted by Jo Ann Starkey)

Grief often lasts longer for parents of a murdered child because of the violence associated with the death. Also, the ensuing legal and justice system hearings, trials, and sentencing keep the death in the forefront. Unfortunately, the parents do not have a real chance to do their grief work until everything is over...if it ever is.

Jim:

"It's never over. Every parole hearing for Charles Moore, I'm there to make sure he doesn't get out."

Kim's Story:

My friend, Lisa, and I left Dallas in high spirits on July 23, 2010, heading for a bachelorette party in New Braunfels, Texas that was being held for another friend, also named Lisa. We were all quite close, as the two "Lisas" had been my bridesmaids just eight months before in Florida where I had married my sweetheart, Lance, at a softball tour-

nament. Softball has always been important in my life, and we had actually met at one of these tournaments. Prior to this, I had been divorced for twenty years and *my children were my life.*

Lisa and I arrived in New Braunfels in time to get settled, have dinner, and go to a few clubs before coming back to our rented house and playing

**Gift for big Tony Romo fan.
Last Christmas**

Kim and Patrick

Patrick's last birthday

147

bachelorette games. We planned to float the near-by Guadalupe River in old bridesmaid dresses the next morning.

The phone call that changed my life forever came at 4:30 am from Lance. He was crying and said, "Hon, I hate to tell you, but you have to come home right now."

My heart was beating tremendously as I fearfully asked "Why?"

Lance said he didn't know the details yet, but Patrick, my twenty-three-year-old son, had been shot. I asked him to go to the hospital right away so Patrick would not be alone.

I started throwing things into my bag. The room was dark and I trampled over others, telling them I had to go. When I made it to the car - no keys. I finally remembered that I had removed them from my purse the night before so I wouldn't lose them. When I made it back to the car, the bride-to-be's sister was in the driver's seat. They had no intention of letting me drive. Then, Lisa took her place and we headed home to Dallas, a ride that seemed to take forever.

As soon as we left New Braunfels, I began texting everyone I knew who prays to pray for Patrick. I frantically tried to find out about his condition, but my family and friends knew little and were on their way to the hospital. I talked with the hospital and was told that Patrick was on life support.

We finally arrived at the hospital and everyone from my family was there. Lance led me into the hospital room and there lay my Patrick. On one side, he appeared to be sleeping; on the other was a large bandage. We always had a family song as the kids grew up entitled *Life is Precious, Life is Sweet* by Wes King. I have it on my I-Phone and started playing and singing it. A single tear rolled out of Patrick's eye. I like to think that it was from God and Patrick – they gave me that tear.

"Life is Precious, Life is Sweet,
Like the earth beneath my feet,
Though I know I'm passing through,
I know I belong to you."
Wes King, *Common Creed* Album

Later in the day, I met with the brain surgeon and was told that Patrick had been shot point blank in the eye with a .22 caliber pistol, shattering his brain. (I later learned that Patrick had been defending a friend.) The brain surgeon explained to me the difference between coma and brain death. Unfortunately, there was no activity in Patrick's brain – he was brain dead. I made the decision to take him off life support and donate his organs, which gives me the feeling that Patrick is continuing on and benefitting others. But, before doing so, the nurses made two molds of Patrick's hand for me - one of his hand and another of my hand holding his. I treasure these.

At Patrick's funeral, the room was overcrowded, way into the foyer. I had a basketball for all his friends to sign, which is now displayed in my formal dining room. My gifted sister, Debbie, suggested the songs played at his funeral. [Part of the lyrics from some of these songs are scattered throughout this chapter.]

Patrick, being twenty-three, was just finding himself. He wanted to be a fire-fighter like his grandpa. He had such a buoyant personality and was so smart. The world is missing out by not having him here. I'm missing out by not having Patrick and mini Patricks and Patricias here.

Kim:

"Luckily for me, the night after they captured Royce, someone notified me that his bond had been reduced. This infuriated me. The original bond was set at $1 million, but it was now $100,000.00 for the murder of my son and $100,000.00 for a prior sex abuse offense. I immediately met with the prosecuting attorney, and she did get the judge to raise Royce's bond to 500K for murder and 100K for the sex offender charge. Not good enough – but better. He didn't have the money to post bail.

Also, I had to stay on the local police department the whole time to get them to do their job. It was very disheartening."

If loved ones are kept "out of the loop" by the justice system, anger may certainly be heightened, not lessened. Anger may then be felt not only towards the perpetrator of the crime, but also towards the legal system: its perceived ineptness, unfairness and/or slowness. Unfortunately, society does not understand pa-

150

rental grief, period, much less the grief of parents whose child was murdered.

Mother of sixteen-year-old daughter:

"NOTHING seems to matter anymore. All the reasons for living seem to have died with the murder of my daughter. My family doesn't understand my continued hurt and neither do my friends. They seem to think that I should be somewhat *over* it after two and one/half years. The fact that she was murdered, and the law enforcement is not going to do anything - they think I should simply 'jolt' myself into that realization and get on with my life."

Before telling Jim's story, I need to say that after my son's death, I thought there could be no grief as great as that felt by a bereaved parent. However, after taking a counseling position with Hospice, I quickly learned that children who lose a parent have a really difficult time and do not have the mental capacities to work through grief as well as adults. Suicide and homicide prove especially difficult for children and young people.

Jim's Story:

My brothers and I were practically raised in the church – Dad (James) was Minister of Music, and Mom (Chere) was pianist. We never heard them argue, but when I was eleven, they divorced.

The next year, my beautiful mother was raped, shot in the face three times, and left (naked) dead in the back floorboard of her car. Her car was found in an abandoned schoolyard.

I was obsessed with what had happened to her.

Mom (Chere)

1974 Dad, Mom, Oscar,
Jim and Louis

I couldn't think or focus in school. I had horrible pictures in my head of what my mom had suffered, and they wouldn't go away. Plus, I felt so different from my classmates. They treated me as if I had some awful disease. I didn't belong.

Jim today with son Bryce
and wife Marilyn.

Then, when I was thirteen, Dad and two employees who worked for him in a sideline construction business were arrested for Mom's murder. I couldn't believe it. But I knew he didn't do it. He couldn't! Neither the prosecutors nor the defense attorneys would tell me anything for fear I would tell my father, and I probably would have.

When I was sixteen, Dad was convicted of

capital murder and criminal solicitation and sent to death row in Huntsville. He had supposedly hired his employees to kill my mother while he was out of town. I was devastated.

My brothers and I bounced around between families until we finally found a relatively stable home life with my grandparents. Then, four years later, when I was twenty, a secretary to the prosecutor came forward and said, "There are some men on death row that do not belong there." Evidently, the D.A. had altered evidence in my dad's trial, so Dad was to be given a new trial. However, the trial would not take place for another four years. All this time, our lives seemed to be on hold, but the second trial finally started.

One of the twelve jurors was convinced that Dad was guilty. He would not give in, so the jury compromised. Dad was convicted but for a lesser offense. Because of all the time he had already spent on death row, he would be out in one week. I was SO excited. My wife and I made arrangements for Dad to live with us, but I still had questions. Having always been a detail minded, organized person, I made out a list of questions I wanted Dad to answer, primarily about Mom. So, I excitedly struck off to see Dad with my list.

I asked Dad a few questions, but after a few minutes, he said, "Jim, I did it, and she deserved it."

I was totally shocked and dumbfounded! Could NOT believe it. I had spent all this time believing in his innocence. He wasn't sorry, and he was blaming her! I was *furious.* "You will never see us again. I'm going to do everything I can to see that you spend the rest of your life in jail."

The media can work with you or against you. I used the media to put out a plea for the public to write letters to deny my father's parole. They responded, and he was sent to the Ellis Unit at Huntsville and faced life in prison.

I later had a son and did visit Dad again. He had changed. At first, I thought he had "found religion" like inmates say they do. But he truly had changed. He apologized, and for the first time, accepted responsibility for the crime. "Jim. I'm so sorry for what I did to you, your brothers and your mother."

I asked him "How did this happen, Dad? How did you go from being a Christian family man to a killer?" He said it all came down to choices. In his sideline construction business, he started going to bars with his employees. (A choice) He had an affair. (A choice) Mom knew this but the last straw for her was when he hit her. That's when they divorced.

Then, one afternoon while drinking with his employees, he casually mentioned that he wished his wife were dead. So that choice was soon made.

Then, if she were to die anyway, he might as well profit from it so he could "be free and live the good life," so he took out life insurance. The planning progressed. His two employees were going to "do the deed" while he was out of town.

In my quest for *facts,* I went to see Charles

154

Moore, "the shooter." There, I suffered yet another betrayal. The killers were supposed to kill Mom AND my brothers and me. (More insurance money.) The two men had Mom in the car and drove around looking for us, but Mom would not tell them where we were. She told them we were with our father, knowing we were not. There is no telling the indignities, abuse and pain she suffered to protect us. She saved our lives. She suffered horribly herself so that we might live.

I learned more about choices when Charles Moore told me this. My choices. When he told me this, I wanted to hurt him. *Really* hurt him. At one point, I wanted to kill him, like he had killed my mom. I wanted to strangle that little old man, and it seemed the logical, rational thing to do at that moment. But, in those few seconds, I realized I had a choice, and I chose to get up and walk away.

I now believe that whether we have one second or two hours to make a choice, it is still ours to make. However, my mother and your children did not have the opportunity to make a choice about whether they lived or died. Someone else made that choice.

My father did change. He died in prison and the warden called to tell us that they wanted to have the first-ever inmate funeral in the prison. We didn't particularly want to attend, but we thought, "One last thing and it's over." When we arrived, we walked down a long hall to the chapel. The first-ever men's chorus (started by my father)

began the service. Afterwards, three hundred inmates walked up, one by one, shook our hands
and said, "I became a Christian because your Dad
shared Christ with me." It was overwhelming.
My brothers and I were finally able to let go of the
hurt, bitterness, and anger we had been carrying
around with us as we left the prison gate.

Steve also talked about choices:
"...A part of life that I do not understand...
When someone has choices, WHY would they
make the worse possible choice?"

With homicide, a family's grief is often placed on hold until
the perpetrator of the crime is apprehended – and tried – and sentenced by the justice system. Delay after delay may occur, causing much frustration and anger.

Jim:
"I really did not grieve Mom's death until after
Dad confessed. Until that time, I focused on get-
ting Dad out of jail."

Emphasis is placed on the perpetrator(s) of the crime, the law-
yers and judges, but the VICTIMS are often forgotten as they
desperately seek answers to the *why's* and *how's* of the crime.

Jim:
"Everything in the news was about Dad's trial.
Mom was never mentioned."

Also, the victims may be further victimized in the trial. Ro-

156

berta Roper, mother of Stephany, expressed this in a talk she gave on *Murdered Children*.[2]

> "We were very naive in 1982. We would learn from witnesses that Stephany's character was called into question. Why was she out at that time of night? How many drinks had she had in the course of the evening? Why was she alone? What was she wearing? – all of those things that any rape victim and any victim of any violence encounters when they become a victim of someone else's choices."

The defense attorneys often paint the perpetrator of the crime as a wonderful person, desperately needed by his/her family. Witness after witness may come forward, giving the killer wonderful character references, while little may be said about the victim. Or even worse, the victim may be portrayed as someone almost asking for trouble.

Mother of Stephanie:

> "In contrast to the absence of anyone who spoke for Stephanie or the consequences of the crime for which two men have now been convicted, the State heard Jack Ronald Jones plead for his life, ask for mercy, have his father, his wife, his former employer, his child's first grade teacher, his jail-house minister, all take the stand and say that he should be treated with mercy, that he didn't have a history of violence and he had received religion, he had found God, and that he was extremely remorseful. I guess the final one that was

the real blow in my mind is that if he were to be
sentenced harshly, it would cause lifelong anguish
to his family."

One of the horrors experienced by those whose loved one was
murdered are the questions: "Did my loved one suffer?" "How
long did she live with the knowledge that she was going to die?"
"Were her last hours, minutes, seconds lived in absolute terror,
knowing that her death was imminent?"

Jim:

"I was obsessed with what happened to Mom.
How long did she have to ride around, knowing
she was going to die? What additional atroci-
ties did she suffer besides being raped and killed?
How long did my mom suffer?"

Fantasies of revenge may accompany the usual grief symptoms. This is common and may even be helpful in releasing some
of the anger and frustration felt. [1]

Jim:

"I had thoughts of how I could kill all of them.
I wanted all three to get the DEATH sentence.
None received the death penalty. The shooter is
now serving life."

Steve:

"Early on, I fantasized that someone would
hold something over my ex-wife's face to show
her how it felt to not be able to breathe, to experience the terror of believing she was going to die;

158

then remove it before she actually died. I wanted her to experience the feelings and fears that Kelsey must have felt."

Just as Jim said he felt *different,* didn't belong and had problems in school, most parents of a murdered child feel much social stigma. Its almost as if others think it's *catching,* or that there is some reason this happened to you, not them. They're safe from such things. Consequently, the grieving person may feel very alone and stigmatized in their grief.

Steve:

"Early on, I realized that I had to find and be among people who <u>understood</u> what I was going through, so I wouldn't feel like such a weirdo. I found Parents Of Murdered Children, Inc., The Compassionate Friends and Our Garden of Angels. They understood. Socializing has been MOST difficult. I even keep my distance from neighbors. I would rather they just know me as the guy next door, rather than the guy whose daughter was murdered.

When I date, I don't know what or how much to tell my date. When asked, 'Do you have children?' I usually just say 'I had one daughter, and she's now in Heaven.' It's awkward. How much do I tell?"

Jim:

"We were treated poorly as victim's kids. But when my father was indicted, we were treated *very* unkindly, not only by kids, but also by teachers

159

and law enforcement...everyone."

So, what helps?
    Steve:

        "I realized that forgiveness towards my ex-wife had to take place...not for her, but for me. Even though she was no longer around, she was controlling my feelings and feeding my anger and revengeful feelings through my resentment of her. I wanted to enjoy life again, and to do that, I had to release this burden. I had to find forgiveness for my own benefit. I didn't want this to hang over my head for the rest of my life."

    Jim:

        "I did finally forgive my father. When I went to see 'the shooter,' he asked me to forgive him, but I could not at that time. In a couple of weeks, however, I wrote to him, telling him that I did forgive him.

        Forgiveness wasn't a sudden decision; it was a process."

    I have heard the analogy that by allowing your life to be filled with hate and revenge is like filling a vessel with acid. The acid eats away at the vessel containing it, eventually destroying the vessel itself. Perhaps some feel, as these men did, that they could not carry this burden; it would destroy them, ruining their own chances for happiness.

    Others may feel that forgiveness is not possible or even desirable, especially early on in their grief.

160

Part of Kim's Victim Impact Statement:

"There's no way you'll ever know the full extent of the pain you've caused. Not just to Whitney and me...as devastated as we are...but to his grandparents, aunts, uncle, cousins, nieces, nephews, my husband...and people who called him [Patrick} their friend...

Although I'm a Christian, I hold on to my worldly ways right now as I can tell you that I can't forgive you. I can honestly say that this may be one thing that I may never be able to do. I've never hated anyone, and I do not feel hatred towards you, but your name and forgiveness do not flow in my vocabulary at the same time.

I'm so full of pain and anger that I don't know if I ever want to get to a point of forgiveness. Some people say that in order to press forward I'll need to forgive you. That anger and hurt is what's pressing me forward. Your choice to take my son's life was your choice, and I hope that you pay dearly for that. My choice is to make sure Patrick lives on. And know this, Royce!....HE WILL LIVE ON. I will be his voice...although you killed a part of me that day, you've also stirred up a passion within me to keep him alive."

So What Else Helps?
Jim:

"Talk about it! Talk about your loss, your anger, frustrations – all your feelings. Tell your story, over and over if necessary."

By expressing our feelings, we release them. Not all at once, but eventually, we do not HAVE to tell our story anymore … or as often. A little of our grief comes out with each and every telling.

Steve:

"I have a theory that **"The Five 'F's'"** help me.

1. <u>Faith</u>. I kept asking, 'What is my purpose now?' If there is no meaning to life other than spending time on earth, then we spend the rest of our days in anger and sadness. I believe our purpose on earth is to love and serve others.

2. & 3. <u>Family and Friends</u>. We need loving support, even if we have to ask for it. We may have to educate our family and friends on how they can help us.

4. <u>Future</u>. Look towards the future rather than living in our past. I once heard a speaker say that we're like a car with a front windshield (our future) and a rear-view mirror (our past). What lies ahead is so much larger, just as a car's front windshield is so much larger, and we need to focus on that instead of our past. I try to do that.

5. <u>Forgiveness</u>. I struggled with forgiveness for a long time. I was saying the Lord's Prayer every day, '…Forgive us our trespasses as we forgive those who trespass against us.' I realized that I was not practicing what I was praying. I found it necessary to forgive my ex-wife, although I realize this isn't for everyone."

Jo Ann:

"What helped me? Cry, weep, scream, moan …whatever is necessary. Crying is not a strong enough word. In addition to crying, I needed such words as *'wailing, moaning, groaning and screaming.'* I experienced these emotions or feelings (whatever they are) quite frequently, even though this was totally out of character for me. I am not an overly emotional person, but I found many times when I was alone in my car that the tears would turn into loud wailing and groaning. That seemed to be the only way I could release the horrific pain I was feeling....I sounded like a terribly injured animal."

We did not have a choice about what happened to our loved one. That choice was taken from us by another. However, we do have a choice about how we live the rest of our lives. We can live in anger, resentment and pain, be forever destroyed by what has happened to us, or we can choose to <u>survive</u> first, and then learn to live our new lives and actually find joy again.

However, we must do our grief work. It doesn't go away because we avoid it…it simply manifests itself in other ways such as illnesses. Neither does it go away with time alone. We have to work with time. One thing that seems to help is to use our newfound knowledge of our own pain to help others; by helping others, we help ourselves.

Reinvestments:

At first, we are too overwhelmed to think of ways we can honor our deceased child, but nearly all bereaved parents eventually feel compelled to honor their child or loved one in some way–to make something positive come from the death. Some play an active role in support groups, like Jo Ann; some find ways to fight the system, to make it better for others down the road, like Kim. We each have our own talents and abilities.

This chapter would not have been possible without Jo Ann. Not only did she let others know that I was searching for people to interview, she worked with me throughout the book, proofreading and doing whatever she could do to help – sometimes just pepping me up and giving me courage.

One of her greatest contributions is reaching out to families of murdered children. Jo Ann makes presentations to universities, churches, Criminal Justice Systems and other groups to tell about the traumatic effects of crime on individuals, families and neighborhoods. She and Jim both serve on Victim Impact Panels that go into prisons and tell their stories to violent offenders. Hearing the impact that violence has on the victims helps the offenders to build empathy for others, including their previous victims. Consequently, they are less likely to offend in the future.

To be so newly bereaved (seven months when I wrote this), Kim has accomplished much. She is responsible for a bill being passed by the House that all violent offenders not be allowed parole. It did not pass the Senate this year, but she will fight until it does. This weekend, we attended a wine tasting event she sponsored to make money for the Patrick Nunnelly Scholarship Fund and for organ donation.

Early in his grief, Steve organized a fund raiser to build a gazebo in a park that's near the cemetery where Kelsey is buried. Each year, he gives a Kelsey Marie Roberts College Scholarship to a graduating Keller High School student and will continue to do so until Kelsey would have graduated. He participates in 5K runs for various organizations where he always wears a *Remember Kelsey* T-shirt.

Jim received both the 2007 Dallas Cowboys Community

Quarterback Award and the 2008 Texas Governor's Volunteer of the Year Service Award from Governor Rick Perry for his work in the Bridges to Life program, a non-profit Texas prison system program that facilitates face to face meetings between violent offenders and victims of violent crimes. The inmates taking part in the fourteen week program do exercises in workbooks and hear victims tell how violent acts affected their lives. Apparently the program works, because the recidivism rate of violent offenders that have completed the program is only 11% to 15% while the rate for violent offenders that have not completed the program is about 80%. Bridges to Life not only helps offenders make more positive choices in their lives, it also helps the victims heal from their psychological wounds. Jim also donates time to victim impact panels for Victim Services, Dallas County Commission and both the Dallas County and Tarrant County Juvenile Justice Departments.

Roberta Roper has fought hard for victim's rights since their daughter, Stephanie, was slain in 1982. She and her husband, Vincent, founded the Stephanie Roper Committee and Foundation, Inc. where she was executive director until 2002, when it merged into the Maryland Crime Victims' Resource Center, Inc.

Roberta has been recognized by Presidents Reagan (1988) and Clinton (1994) and received their awards for outstanding service to victims of crime. In 2006, she was presented with the *Lifetime Achievement Award* by Governor Robert Ehrlich. In 2006, the Maryland Crime Victims Resource Center, Inc. was honored by the U.S. Justice Deportment, Office for Victims and given the National Crime Victims' Rights Week Award for Professional Innovation in Victim Services. In 2008, she received the Victim Advocate Award from the National Crime Victims Law Institute.

Chapter XIX
Drug Overdose and other Substance Related Deaths

Whether our child's death followed a long-term pattern of addiction or a one-time experimentation, the pain has been excruciating. When our children were young, we typically could "fix" our child's ills, but with substance abuse, nothing seemed to work. As one mother stated, "We had no control, and they had no control."

Jacob's Mom:
> "I tried buying phone cards – not buying phone cards, trying tough love – not trying tough love. Nothing worked."

Our child likely *wanted* to quit drugs or alcohol, but despite our pleadings, threats, bribes – they could not. Alcohol and/or drugs had relentlessly taken over their minds and bodies, and we didn't have a chance.

> "The addict has little or no control because the parts of the brain responsible for decision making and impulse regulation are damaged by the drugs, making it very difficult for the addict to choose NOT to be an addict."[1 (p.175)]
>
> Gabor Mate, M.D.
> A foremost authority on drug addiction
> Author of *In the Realm of Hungry Ghosts*

Andy, Recovering Addict:

"Meth grabbed me by the balls and never let go. Even though I've been drug free for a year, it's a daily struggle. The lure of drugs promises heights of ecstasy, but, in reality, they deliver the pits of Hell."

As parents, when we first suspected that our child was experimenting or addicted to drugs, we likely felt fear and anger – fear for our child and anger at both the child for their substance abuse and possibly ourselves for not recognizing the symptoms or realizing the severity of the problem sooner. It was difficult to admit that our child could have a problem. Wouldn't our child be smarter than that? Didn't we warn them about drugs? What went wrong? (Some parents in the survey sought help immediately, but their outcome was the same.)

Jen's Mom:

"I suspected within a short time that my daughter was using drugs. Some of the signs were there, like a change in personality and a change in friends. I talked with her, but of course, she denied it. I tried talking with my husband, asking that we work as a team in dealing with this, but he denied that she was using. Years later, my daughter admitted that I had been absolutely right; this was the beginning of her using drugs ...and, actually, the beginning of the end."

The teen years are a time of moodiness and volatility, and it's hard to tell the difference between substance abuse and typical teen behavior. While our teen or young adult may have thought they were "all grown up" when they experimented with drugs and/or alcohol, recent research indicates that a young person's brain simply does not reach maturity until the mid 20's. Part of their brain is mature – the part where impulses to act originate. However, the part that controls those impulses and balances risk and reward does not mature until the mid 20's, and this is the part of the brain that determines how much priority is given to messages like *Do it now,* versus *What are the consequences?* [2] (pp. 63-70) Drug use delays this maturation even longer. (For more information on this subject, see "Teenagers and Young Adults" in the "Suicide" chapter.)

Most parents whose child died due to the disease of addiction not only grieve after the child's death, they have suffered and grieved since the day that drugs entered and changed their child's life – and their own. Everyone suffered. The child seemed to have had a dual personality; one lovable and kind, the other, manipulative, devious, and uncaring. Parents wanted to believe the lovable side was the true personality, but unfortunately, the two personalities were two sides of the same coin.

We felt extreme frustration when we saw our child make terrible, self-destructive decisions, yet our attempts to help were usually met with denial, anger and desperate attempts to manipulate and persuade. Even so, after a child's death, we tend to run scenarios of things we might have said or done differently, wondering if anything could have changed our child's fate. *Maybe if we had been tougher, or more of a friend, or tried another treatment center* – the list often goes on and on. Many parents had struggled with their child through a lengthy history of addiction, rehabs, hope, and back to addiction. They've heard promises, lies, had calls from jail, seen their child sick, and prayed many times that their child would live through the day or night.

Mother:

"At first, I was horrified to learn that my child was in jail, but later, I would feel such relief. I knew where he was. He was safe, being fed, and drugs usually were not in the picture. I wouldn't have to worry for awhile. I could sleep."

Even though we tried everything we knew to get our child off drugs, we still tend to chastise ourselves for not somehow saving our child. Professionals have no one answer, no sure treatment, but we think we should have known.

While it is natural for the loved one of an addict to wish to reform him, it seldom can be done. The addict has to make the decision to give up drugs, and it's no easy task.

Andy, Recovering Addict:

"The lure of a euphoric high is so great that nothing must stand in its way. I've gone into total rages against anyone and everyone that kept me from getting a high. Also, nothing will make the guilt of past deeds go away except another *hit*."

You likely witnessed your child's suffering and heard them cry out in pain and desperation because they could not *kick the habit,* but apparently kicking the habit isn't easy. Why is the seduction of some drugs so immediate and addicting? According to Dr. Mate, we all have natural opiate/endorphins in the brain that serve many purposes. Sometimes they reduce pain, both physical and mental, sometimes they give us a "natural high." For example, eating a good meal can increase the presence of dopamine in the synaptic spaces of the brain by 50%, sexual activity – by 100%. However *"none of these can compete with cocaine, which more than triples dopamine levels. Yet cocaine is a miser, compared with crystal meth whose dopamine-enhancing effect is an astounding 1,200%."* [1 (p. 154)]

Your whole family probably experienced tremendous trauma, heartbreak, and even open hostility from your child as you desperately sought help. Financial burdens may have sky-rocketed and homes refinanced to pay for "one more treatment," usually to no avail. The precious but addicted child was never far from your mind. *Is he/she OK? Is he using again? Is she safe and warm?* The child may have created havoc for years. It's no wonder that parents may feel a temporary relief after the child's death. The drama and fears for their child are over, and the worse thing that can happen has already happened. The dreaded phone call finally came.

Steve's Mom:

"Fearing the phone call? Was it a relief? At times I thought it would be – just let it be over. But now, **NO!** There was hope with the misery before. Now it is only loss and misery. The pain never ends. I know I will not hear his voice on the other end of the phone. I will not have his arms around me again. We shared the same sick sense of humor that no one gets or understands. Though I thought it might be a relief, it certainly is not."

Steve

As parents, we desperately miss our child, but not the disease of addiction. As one mother shared, "There is no depth great enough to measure the pain we have felt." Unfortunately, we also feel much stigma because of our child's addiction and/or drug related death.

Steve's Mom:

"I did not want my closest friends to know my son was an addict! I hated not being able to share the most painful and dominating part of my life. Part of it was shame. But a bigger part is the ignorance, or better words may be the lack of education concerning addiction. There is so much prejudice and judgment. I heard so many comments about others – '*Just a drug addict.*' '*Would not want an addict visiting our neighborhood. No one would be safe.*' '*They all need to be locked up.*' My own brother who loved my son, said '*He needs to grow up.*' People do not understand the disease."

We never stopped loving our child. We first knew him or her as a loving, caring, perhaps mischievous individual. It was later that drugs entered the picture and started our son or daughter on a downward spiral, out of our reach. Unfortunately, other people often do not remember the good qualities in our child; they only think of the drug-induced sad ending and think *"that's all they were,"* but we know better.

Steve's Mom:

"One is not 'just an addict.' They are someone's child, sibling, mother, father or friend. It is possible for them to be a *good* person with a very *bad* problem."

Parents whose child(ren) have died from substance-related causes are some of the strongest, most intelligent, yet most compassionate parents ever. They've dealt with issues that, luckily, most humans never face. Furthermore, for many, their child's death came after years of excruciating pain and frustration for both themselves and their child. Even so, as parents, we often find ways to indict and condemn ourselves for our child's death.

I was introduced to the story of the Two Arrows by Barbara Allen in her "Shatter the Stigma" workshop.

Story of the Two Arrows:
(Adapted from a 2500-year-old story
attributed to The Budda)

The first arrow, in this story, represents any misfortune, slight, or injury that causes us mental or physical pain. In our case, life has thrust a terrible arrow into us – the death of our beloved child which has wounded us to the core. However, the second arrow, or arrows, are those we inflict into ourselves. These are the "should haves" and "Why didn't I's?" that may represent decades of previously held beliefs and assumptions we now have to challenge. We often immerse ourselves in self-criticism and guilt for things we did or did not do, even though we tried everything we knew at the time. While this is probably true for all bereaved parents, it is likely that few deaths cause this self-questioning and criticism as much as drug overdose and suicide.

**So, what can we do to help ourselves and not inflict
more arrows of pain into ourselves?**

Although we could not prevent the death of our precious child, we can stop inflicting more secondary arrows into ourselves. Our cultural upbringing, norms, and values cause responses that take only a millisecond to spring into (re)action.

These are our deeply held "oughts" and "shoulds" that appear to be in control of us – as if the tail is wagging the dog. We have to challenge some of our former beliefs, like the myth of perfect parenthood discussed in Chapter II. Do we punish ourselves for things we know now that we had no way of knowing at the time? When professionals aren't always sure of the best treatment for drug-addicted patients, why should we have known exactly what to do? Yes, we likely made mistakes and said things we wish we had not said, but we always had our child's best interest at heart. We need to examine our self-criticisms and focus on what we did do right and realize that our child's downward spiral was totally out of our control.

You didn't cause it,

You can't control it,

And you can't cure it.

…Al Anon

Dealing with a substance abusing child is not for the faint of heart. Your suffering has known no boundaries, but you will get stronger and life will be good again, though this may not seem to be possible at this time. So, hold your head high and understand that you have tremendous inner strength and abilities that you may not even know you possess, but they will shine through. Give yourself time – and love.

_____**No shame or blame ~ Just love**©*

* From bracelet given by Barbara Allen in her "Shatter the Stigma" workshop. The National Compassionate Friends Convention, 2013

Chapter XX
AIDS
Acquired Immunodeficiency Syndrome

Many of our children's deaths carry a note of stigma, or a mark of shame that is placed by society on the death, but AIDS is one of the worse. Acquaintances and friends do not know how to approach the subject - so they don't. As a result, the parents are often alone in their grief.

Regardless of how AIDS is acquired, it is one of the most devastating diseases for the parents, child and care-givers to bear. While many advances have been made, and the HIV virus is no longer inevitably fatal, [1 (p. 2)] these advances may have been too little, too late for our child.

Prior to the HIV diagnosis, many parents had already suffered much grief because the lifestyle chosen by their child was different than their own. Discussed below will be homosexuality, intravenous drug use, heterosexual transmission, infection due to blood products, and mother to baby transmission.

Homosexuality:

Because AIDS was first found among homosexual men, it was initially thought to be a homosexual disease. Of course, the HIV virus was soon discovered in drug users that had shared needles and/or syringes, then hemophiliacs and patients who had received tainted blood products, and finally, in the partners or babies of the above. However, because it was first found in homosexuals, our fears and lack of understanding about homosexuality have greatly colored our response to this epidemic.

It is normal to fear the unknown and to find reasons why something bad has happened to someone else – not us. The *just world assumption* is the belief that the world is a just and fair place; therefore, victims of misfortune must have done something to deserve their fate. This attitude has probably never been more evident than in the early years of AIDS; society wanted to believe that homosexuals had brought this plague on themselves.

The more we learn about homosexuality, the more we realize that homosexuals are people just like us. It is thought that masculinization or feminization occur within the brain before birth, then things happen along the way that influence and/or reinforce which direction we go. The child often has little or no choice. One AIDS-infected young man expressed the following about his homosexuality.

> " I knew that there was something wrong with me, that I wasn't an acceptable human being because I liked men, not women. I prayed for years for God to change me. I didn't want to tell my family for fear they would not love me and would reject me – so I kept the secret." [2]

When discussing whether or not homosexuals actually have a choice about their sexuality, Beverly Barbo, author of *The Walking Wounded,* posed the following questions at a Regional Compassionate Friends Conference:

> "Would you *choose* to have the wrath of God called down upon you by your church and be

175

called immoral?

Would you *choose* to be called sick and perverted by society?

Would you *choose* to have the law call you illegal?

Would you *choose* to have your parents call you...maybe not at all?" [2]

It is usually difficult for parents to accept their child's homosexuality at first, especially if they are from *the old school*.

Father of HIV positive young man:

"I guess I always considered myself a *man's man*. For our son to prefer staying inside instead of going hunting and fishing with me really hurt. I was not a good father. When I finally realized that he was gay, I was angry for a long time.

I wish I could turn back time."

Many parents experience significant anger when they first suspect or find out that their son or daughter is homosexual. *How could my child be this way?* *Our whole family is heterosexual. What will our friends say?* *Do we tell them?* Anger may be directed towards the child, themselves, society, friends that say the wrong thing or forsake them, and/or God. Knowing that their child will have difficulties living in a homophobic society, the parents fear for their child. *Will my child be shunned, despised, considered a throw-away by society?* *Will she/he have a chance for happiness?* And, possibly the sickening question arises: *Will he get AIDS?* The parents may also grieve for the grandchildren they will never have by this child.

In some cases, the religious community appears to cause more suffering than help to AIDS patients and their loved ones.

176

Mother, whose son had AIDS:

"I was in a supermarket when I saw our preacher, so I asked him to pray for James (my son) because he was really sick. When he asked what was wrong and I told him 'AIDS,' he stepped away as if I had slapped him. He just stood there with a horrified, scared look on his face like I might touch him. I turned and walked away and never attended that church again."

Beverly Barbo, in her talk at The Compassionate Friends Conference, discussed how some individuals have a problem realizing that homosexuals can be Christian, just like anyone else.

"So many people can not put the words *Christian* and *homosexual* together in the same sentence because they think of homosexuality only in the terms of lust and sex; never love and caring. But anyone with that mind-set, I would have liked to have taken them to that little cottage in Hollywood, California, and they could have watched Tommy, as he cared for Tim under the most terrible of circumstances, - and that day in the airport, as I watched Tommy almost carry that worn-out hulk of a young man that was my son onto the plane, I thought <u>love</u>." [2]

Many in the religious community now see those infected with HIV and AIDS as fellow human beings we need to accept, love as our neighbor and help if necessary. Definitely not shun.

While medications have been developed for partners of

AIDS infected patients to help prevent them from contracting the AIDS virus, the medication must be faithfully taken.

Injecting Drug Users Who Share Needles:
In the case of needle-infected AIDS, the parents also likely suffered long before the child was diagnosed HIV positive. When the parents first suspected that their child was experimenting or addicted to drugs, the natural reaction would be fear and anger, fear for their child and anger at both the child for their drug use and possibly themselves for not recognizing the symptoms or realizing the severity of the problem sooner. Why didn't I do more?" "We should have tried a treatment center, or one more treatment center," the list often goes on and on. However, many parents have struggled with their child through a lengthy history of addiction, rehabs, hope, and back to addiction. They've heard promises, lies, had calls from jail, seen their child sick from withdrawal, and prayed many times that their child would live through the day or night. The parents probably had tried everything they knew to help the child. Regardless, as parents, we usually find some way to chastise ourselves.

For some, the child's HIV infection may have been a complete surprise since many teenage athletes turn to steroids in an effort to build bigger muscles. Because steroids are illegal, they're sold on the black market, as are the needles needed to inject them. Unfortunately, it is not uncommon for drug pushers to re-package and re-sell used needles. Consequently, the risk of becoming HIV positive or getting other diseases has been added to the other risks of using steroids.

Heterosexuals who infect their partner or others:
The parents may have felt that their child was headed down a treacherous path due to his choice of risk-taking behaviors and friends. If the parent knew that his/her child's partner was an

178

injecting drug user or was bi-sexual, they likely pleaded, "Get out," perhaps to deaf ears. If a parent was aware that his child frequented prostitutes, she/he likely feared that their child would be infected with the HIV virus; or the child may have resorted to prostitution to pay for drugs or as a means of survival. Regardless, as parents, we hurt when our child dies. Also, I don't think we have a clue *how much* we're going to hurt until after their death.

Other sources of the HIV virus:

Hemophiliacs and patients who received blood transfusions or an organ transplant prior to 1985 were at risk of getting the HIV virus, though there is still a slight risk. If your loved one was one of those that slipped through the cracks and received tainted blood products after this time, you may feel tremendous anger towards everyone – the medical community, those with risk-taking behaviors that proliferated the disease – and probably anger at society in general. You may feel *Why me? Why MY beloved child? It's not fair.* And it isn't, just as so much of life isn't, fair.

Other innocent victims are babies that are infected by the HIV virus via the mother's placenta, contact with her blood during delivery, or from her milk. New drugs have now been introduced that *usually* prevent this transmission, but the mother may not be reliable about taking her meds.

Regardless of how AIDS is acquired, the grief must be tremendous when parents first learn that their child is HIV positive. AIDS is not a problem that can be "fixed," like scraped knees or hurt feelings; this horrendous disease is real. However, current advances in medications and technology offer the parent hope: *Maybe a cure will be found in time to save my precious child, or at least, new miracle drugs will help him live a near-normal life.* Unfortunately, even asymptomatic HIV is no bed of roses. Sometimes, our loved-one had been so racked by opportunistic infections that he may have questioned, *"Is it worth the pain and struggle? My life is just...trying to stay alive. I've lost hope."* AIDS-related malignancies, AIDS dementia complex, HIV wasting disease and various infections may occur. All are vicious enemies to the HIV positive patient fighting the battle of his life. Even medications may have wretched and disastrous side effects.

Then, the horrible reality of full-blown AIDS. Hope dwindles with each malicious infection and vile illness. The child's quality of life becomes almost non-existent. Both the parent and child may pray for the child's release from his horrendous suffering, wanting death to be as quick and merciful as possible. If the parent is the primary care-giver, the struggle to keep their child alive for one more day becomes a challenge.

The treatment of HIV positive and AIDS has advanced in great leaps since it was first found in the United States. However, there is still a long way to go, as anyone reading this knows. If your child was in any kind of experimental treatment, then she/he helped others down the line.

Mother to dying son:

Doyle, I hope you can hear me.

I feel so blessed to have had you for my son. You've always been so smart, creative and happy. You've saved so many peoples lives in your nursing career and given them chances for new lives. You've truly been a blessing for all of us.

I've loved you so much. You and I've always had a special connection, and I've cherished it and every minute we've spent together.

I love you,

Mom

Chapter XXI
The Choking Game
&
Auto-Erotic Asphyxiation

While the *desired* purpose of The Choking Game and Auto-Erotic Asphyxiation is different, the temporary result of each is the same: hypoxia, or oxygen starvation to the brain. Unfortunately, the permanent result for both may be brain injury or death. If your child died from either of these or other risk-taking behaviors, the *Teenagers and Young Adults* section in the **Suicide Chapter** of this book will likely be helpful to you.

The Choking Game:
Adolescents often engage in thrill-seeking behaviors, and one of these may be the choking game, also known as *the blackout game, the pass-out game, the scarf game, space monkey, flatlining* and others. The primary goal is to produce a brief euphoric "high," described by participants as a "tingling high," accomplished by reducing blood flow and oxygenation to the brain by means of pressure on the chest, ligatures around the neck, chemicals or bags over the head. The "highs" are actually the brain beginning the process of permanent cell death. Clinicians sometimes call this game "Suffocation Roulette."

Adolescents may play the game for the euphoric high or as a result of peer pressure or a dare. Whether played alone, with a partner, or at a party, this self-induced hypoxia frequently results in the participant losing consciousness. When the victim falls unconscious, the person helping him releases the pressure and the secondary "high" of the oxygen/blood rushing back to the brain is achieved. If the victim is alone and there is no one to release the pressure, the victim's body weight continues to tighten the ligature, usually resulting in death. Even if the victim survives, injuries often include brain damage, seizures, retinal hemorrhaging and/or stroke. [1] (pp. 486-488)

The Choking Game isn't new; variations have been around for generations, though it didn't hit the spotlight until 2005. Anthropologists have recognized Self-Asphyxial Behavior in studies of primitive Celtic cultures, as well as among certain Native Americans and Eskimo children, who engage in risk-taking games involving suffocation called "Smoke Out" and "Red Out." [2] (pp. 303-307)

Unfortunately, the choking game has increased in popularity due to wider visibility on Internet sites and national news shows. [1] (p. 486) Sixty-five videos were found on You-Tube, the popular video-sharing website, portraying adolescents engaging in this activity. These videos basically give others visual "how to" instructions. [3] (pp. 424-425)

It may be some consolation to parents to know that the typical profile of one that participates in the choking game is male, age nine to sixteen, and is usually among the *well-adjusted, high achieving students.*

Auto-erotic Asphyxiation:

The **most** stigmatized death is probably Auto-Erotic Asphyxiation. In fact, parents often choose to say that their child died from suicide, rather than tell the true cause of death. It is believed that many more deaths occur by AEP than is recorded because parents or loved-ones do not want their loved one to be seen in such a compromising position, so they "sanitize" the scene by removing incriminating evidence and dressing or re-dressing their loved one in more "appropriate" clothing. AEP deaths are often

182

ruled suicide" or even "homicide by an unknown person." [4] ^{(pp.}
509-523)

What is auto-erotic asphyxiation? Actually, the choking game and auto-erotic asphyxia are alike in that both use a form of suffocation to achieve the desired result, and both can be lethal. However, the choking game's purpose is to create a euphoric high, while the purpose of AEP is to create sexual arousal or to heighten orgasm. This practice is usually accomplished by self-hanging, though other devices or chemicals may be used.

Death is not the desired result, but because it is usually a solitary act, auto-erotic asphyxia tends to be quite lethal. The individual is usually careful to use some kind of "fail-safe" mechanism to prevent accidental death once they have climaxed, but unfortunately, the "fail-safe" mechanism often fails. The intended strategy is usually a reliance on their own ability to simply stand up from a device lower than they are or remove a plastic bag or mask or chemicals from their head. Unfortunately, not only does the lack of oxygen to the brain cause a light-headed feeling, it also reduces inhibitions making it easy to go too far. As little as seven pounds of pressure will collapse the carotid artery, producing unconsciousness in seconds.

For a parent to find their child hanging or suffocated has to be totally overwhelming and a shock like few others. Normally, there would have been no warning signs that the child was engaging in this activity, no identifying signs of a predisposition to this behavior. The child may have been involved in otherwise healthy relationships, sexual and otherwise. They may even have been committed spouses. As parents, we usually find some way to think "I should have known," but in this case, there were likely no clues.

Parents often wonder, "What do I tell people when they ask how my child died?" When casual acquaintances ask, this is probably one of the many situations when the parent needs a "script," decided upon ahead of time. "It was an accident," and let the person know that the conversation has ended. Or "Suicide," or "We're not sure" or whatever you, the parent, chooses to say. It is your choice. Or, if you want to educate the public, tell the truth. Do what feels best to you at that particular moment. Parents usually develop an almost innate ability to know whom to trust, and whom to avoid. Unfortunately, parents may stay away from support groups – thinking that even support group members would not understand – and there may be some members that do not, but most care about your *hurt*, not how your child died.

Chapter XXII
A Mother's Plight: How Did My Child Die?

Shawn's Story:

My 16-year-old son, Brandtlee, had spent the day at his girlfriend's house, even though I had told him to stay home. The girl's parents, who had made the couple break up about nine months before this, were going to be gone that day, and apparently, Brandtlee and his girlfriend couldn't resist the temptation to be alone together. When he returned home about 6:00 pm, I was quite perturbed with him and told him so. I took away his cell phone for defying me and that was terrible

Brandtlee's Junior year

Brandtlee at 7 years-old

punishment, according to him. But I also told him I loved him.

I had been alone with my boys, Brandtlee and Brandon, since Brandtlee was three and Brandon was seven, so the full weight of the boys' discipline fell on me. However, I had been lucky; both had been easy children – until recently. A few months prior to this, Brandtlee and a group of boys had a scrape with the Carrollton Police Department when they had stayed out past curfew. Also, I had caught him smoking marijuana twice. He was having to be disciplined more than ever, and he sure didn't like it. He was much like a puppy that had seldom been on a leash; he wasn't used to it, and he was fighting it for all he was worth. To have his cell phone taken away was *extreme* punishment.

After fixing himself something to eat, he called his friend, Lance, to tell him that he could not help at the church the next morning because he had school. He then went to his room to watch his new TV that we had just purchased. He also had a computer in his room, so even without his phone, he wasn't cut off from the world.

I was trying to respect Brandtlee's privacy so I didn't check on him until I started to bed about midnight. At that time, I peeked into his room – and the most horrific sight awaited me that will likely haunt my nights and days forever. There, hanging from a cloth belt attached to the lower rod in his closet, was my son, Brandtlee. It was the most ghastly sight I'd ever seen – a sight no

186

mother should ever see.

I frantically tried to get him down but couldn't. I grabbed the phone to call 911 but my fingers jumped all over the phone. Finally, I managed to punch the numbers in correctly, but then I couldn't talk. I managed to say, "<u>Come Here Now</u>!" And they did – almost immediately. Once the police and paramedics arrived, some policemen took me outside to the parking lot while others removed Brandtlee from the closet rod. While in the parking lot, I collapsed. I was conscious, but my muscles just didn't work for awhile. Shock had enveloped me.

Panic, grief, and questions overwhelmed me then and still do. Was this suicide? Brandtlee had laid out his clothes to wear to school the next morning. His backpack, holding completed homework assignments, lay on the bed. His dog, Bam-Bam, was on the window seat. Surely, he wouldn't kill himself in front of his best friend, Bam-Bam, whom he thought was almost human.

About six months before this, he had come home one day and said, "I might as well just kill myself."

I was horrified! "Brandtlee! Why would you say such a thing?"

"Oh, Mom! I'm just pissed off. I don't know why I said that. I'm just mad and didn't really mean it."

Now, I wonder … should I have paid more attention to this? Gotten him counseling? I thought he was just spouting off and having typical teenage problems. He said he didn't mean it. I believed him. Why would he want to kill himself? He was popular in school and was usually a vibrant, happy kid. Things just don't add up.

I initially thought that perhaps he and his girl-friend had argued that day, but, no, that was not the case.

I've heard of "the choking game," but I've questioned his friends, whom I know quite well. I think they're very honest with me, and, apparently, this is not something their group had even thought of doing.

One of the police officers suggested that Brandtlee might have been experimenting with auto-erotic asphyxia, but there were no signs of that. Brandtlee was fully dressed in the jeans and shirt he'd worn that day, and from what I've read about auto-erotic asphyxiation, that would be highly unusual. No porn or fantasy materials were nearby – another sign of AEP. However, he was hanging from the lower closet rod, indicating that he may have intended to simply stand up to loosen the ligature after achieving the desired result. Or maybe he did that in case he changed his mind about suicide. I checked his computer to see what sites he had visited or deleted – but there were none that pertained to the choking game or autoerotic asphyxia.

Had he previously smoked something in a marijuana cigarette, knowingly or unknowingly, besides marijuana? I definitely do not think so, but I also believe that marijuana is a gateway to harder drugs. I understand that methamphetamine depletes certain neurotransmitters in the brain, leaving its victims severely depressed for some time. Could this have been the problem? But I *know* he had not been smoking much marijuana; I would have smelled it.

So how did my son die? I'll likely never know for sure. One day I think one thing, and the next, I think another. However, right now, I believe he was contemplating suicide and decided to see how he would do it, then tried to get loose but couldn't. The toxicology report showed no trace of drugs or alcohol in his system. If he were serious about suicide, wouldn't he use something to give him courage? I just don't understand.

Regardless of how Brandtlee died, his death was so useless because he had such a bright future in front of him. His goal was to be a policeman or fireman, though he was so talented at art and architecture. I will miss and love him always – you can't share 16 years of love, laughter and pain and not have it stay with you forever.

Brandtlee, my son
Brandtlee, you will be in my heart for
as long as I live. Just because your heart has
stopped beating, doesn't mean mine
has stopped loving you.

Love, Mom

Chapter XXIII
Every Exit is Also an Entrance

You and I have exited a doorway, leaving behind our comfortable, familiar past, and for this we mourn. But we are also at the threshold of a new realm of life, a new beginning. We will miss our child and he/she will be a part of us forever, but new joys, new people, new interests will enter our lives in time, giving us the *potential* for new happiness.

However, we must remember that we do not *reap* and *sow* in the same day. Nor does time alone heal our broken hearts; we must work with time. All those painful emotions must be worked through, bit by bit, or perhaps, tear by tear. Finally, one day we find that we not only want to **survive**, we want to **live.** We realize that, yes, yesterday **is** gone, but today is a whole new day. We have exited the doorway of our treasured past, but we're entering a doorway of new horizons, of new beginnings.

Parable of the Twins

Once upon a time, twin boys were conceived in the same womb. Weeks passed and the twins developed. As their awareness grew, they laughed for joy. "Isn't it great to be alive?"

Together the twins explored their world. When they found their mother's cord that gave them life, they sang for joy: "How great is our mother's love that she shares her own life with us!"

As weeks stretched into months the twins noticed how much each was changing. "What does it mean?" asked the one.

"It means that our stay in this world is drawing to an end," said the other one.

"But I don't want to go, I want to stay here always."

"We have no choice," said the other.

"But maybe there is life after birth!"

"But how can that be?" responded the one. "We will shed our life cord, and how is life possible without it? Besides, we have seen evidence that others were here before us, and none of them have returned to tell us that there is life after birth. No, this is the end."

And so the one fell into deep despair, saying: "If conception ends in birth, what is the purpose of life in the womb? It's meaningless! Maybe there is no mother after all."

"But there has to be," protested the other. "How else did we get here? How do we remain alive?"

"Have you ever seen our mother?" said the one. "Maybe she lives only in our minds. Maybe we made her up because the idea made us feel good."

And so the last days in the womb were filled with deep questioning and fear. Finally, the moment of birth arrived. When the twins had passed from their world, they opened their eyes and they cried. For what they saw exceeded their fondest dreams.

Author Unknown

1 Corinthians 2:9
Eye has not seen,
Ear has not heard,
Nor has it so much
As dawned on man
What God had prepared
For those who love him.

Endnotes (References)

Chapter I: Our Story: My Son & I

Chapter II: Physical Symptoms of Grief

1. Li, J., Precht, D. H., Mortensen, P. B., & Olsen, J. (2003). Mortality in parents after the death of a child in Denmark: a nationwide follow-up study. *Lancet*, 363-367.

Chapter III: Phases of Grief

1. Kubler-Ross, E. (1969). *On Death and Dying*. New York: Collier Books, Macmillan Publishing Company. 38-147.

2. Rando, T. A. (1986). The unique issues and impact of the death of a child. In T. A. Rando (Ed.), *Parental Loss of a Child*. Champaign, IL: Research Press. 5-43.

Chapter IV: Anger

1. Gerner, M. (2010, March/April). Grief and your health. *The Compassionate Friends Newsletter, San Angelo, TX*. p. 5.

2. Murray, C. (Speaker). (1989). *Sudden and Accidental Death* (Cassette Recording No. VT-16.) Oakbrook, IL: The Compassionate Friends.

Chapter V: Guilt

1. Gerner, M. (2006, January/February). The myth of perfect parenthood. *The Compassionate Friends Newsletter*. Independence, MO. 5.

2. Miles, M. S. & Demi, A. S. (1986). Guilt in bereaved par-

ents. In T. A. Rando (Ed.), *Parental Loss of a Child*. Champaign, IL: Research Press. 97-118.

3.   Burns, D. D., Combs, D., & Galindo, J. (1992). *Healing the Broken Heart Conference.*

4.   Claypool, J. (Speaker). (1989). *Keynote address* (Cassette Recording). Oakbrook, IL: The Compassionate Friends.

5.   Kushner, H. S. (1981). *When Bad Things Happen to Good People*. New York: Anchor Books.

Chapter VI: Depression

Chapter VII: Fear and Anxiety

Chapter VIII: Grief Characteristics Common to All Bereaved Parents

Chapter IX: Stigmatized Deaths

1.   Houck, J. A. (2007). A comparison of grief reactions in cancer. HIV/AIDS, and suicide bereavement. *Journal of HIV/ AIDS & Social Services. 7(3)*. New York: The Haworth-Press.

Chapter X: Mothers' and Fathers' Grief

1.   Hauser, S. T., Powers, S. I., Weiss-Perry, B., Follansbee, D. J., Rajapark, D. & Green, W. M. (1987). The constraining and enabling coding system manual. Unpublished manuscript.

2.   Jacoby, E. E. (1990) Gender and relationships. <u>American Psychologist, 4,</u> 513-520.

3.   Cole, B. C., (1993). *The Relationship Between Parental Bereavement Reaction Factors and Selected Psychosocial Variables: an Exploratory Study. 4-6, 55-73. Thesis.*

4. Schatz, W. H., (1986). Grief of fathers. In T. A. Rando (Ed.), *Parental Loss of a Child*, Champaign, IL: Research Press, pp. 294-295.

5. Rando, T. A. (1986). The unique issues and impact of the death of a child. In T. A. Rando (Ed.). *Parental Loss of a Child* (6-9). Champaign, IL: Research Press.

Chapter XI: Finding Happiness Again

1. Simms, D. (Speaker). (1986). <u>Banquet Speaker</u> (Cassette Recording No. 8655). Omaha, NE: The Compassionate Friends.

Chapter XII: Gifts from our Child

1. Kübler-Ross, E. (1983). *On Children and Death*. New York, NY: Simon & Schuster. P. 49

Part 2:

Chapter XIII: Miscarriage, Stillbirth, & Early Infant Death

Chapter XIV: SIDS

1. Dyregrov, A., & Matthiesen, S. B. (1987b). Stillbirth, neonatal death and sudden infant death (SIDS): Parental reactions. *Scandinavian Journal of Psychology, 28,* 104-114.

Chapter XV: Death Following Long Term Illness

Chapter XVI: Sudden Death

Chapter XVI: Suicide

1. Giedd, J. N. (2010). The Teen Brain. In D. Gordon, (Ed.) *Cerebrum, Emerging Ideas in Brain Science,* 62-70. Washington DC: Dana Press.

2. Steinberg, L. (2011). *You and Your Adolescent. The Essential Guide for Ages 10-25.* New York: Simon & Schuster.

3. Steinberg, L. (2007). Scientists: Teen brain still maturing. The Washington Post. Retrieved from http://www.washingtonpost.com/wp-dyn/content/article/2007/12/02/AR2007120200809.html

4. Fassler, D. (2007). Scientists: Teen brain still maturing. The Washington Post. Retrieved from http://www.washingtonpost.com/wp-dyn/content/article/2007/12/02/AR2007120200809.html Retrieved from CBS news.com/stories/2007/12 health/main 346047.shtml.

5. Bolton, I. (1981, Winter). When your child has died by suicide. *The Compassionate Friends Newsletter*, 4, 1-5.

6. Joiner, T. E., Van Orden, K. A., Witte, T. K., & Rudd, D. (2009). *The Interpersonal Theory of suicide.* Washington, DC: American Psychological Association.

7. Tucker, P. (February, 1999). Substance abuse and suicidality. *Australasian Psychiatry*, 23 -24.

8. Brent, D. A. (1995). Risk factors for adolescent suicide and suicidal behavior: mental and substance abuse disorders, family, environmental factors and life stress. *Suicide Life Threatening Behavior 25:* 52-63.

9. Betry, C., Etievant, A., Oosterhof, C., Ebert, B., Sanchez, C., & Haddjeri, N. (2011). Role of 5-HT3 receptors in the antidepressant response. *Pharmaceuticals 4.* pp. 603-629.

10. *American Foundation for Suicide Prevention.* (2008). S. I.: American Foundation for Suicide Prevention http://www.afsp.org/.

11. Peale, N. V. (1966). *The Healing of Sorrow.* Pawling, N. Y.: Inspirational Book Service. pp. 34-35.

Chapter XVIII: Homicide

1. Harris, J. S. (2001). *Murder; This Could Never Happen to Me.* p. 7. Austin, TX: Office of the Governor, Criminal Justice Division.

2. Roper, R. (1993). *Death by Homicide.* (Cassette Recording). Reston, VA., Alive Alone National Conference.

Chapter XIX: Drug Overdose

1. Mate, G. (2010). *In the Realm of Hungry Ghosts.* Berkeley, CA: North Atlantic Books.

2. Giedd, J. N. (2010). The Teen Brain. In D. Gordon, (Ed.) *Cerebrum, Emerging Ideas in Brain Science, 62-70.* Washington DC: Dana Press.

Chapter XX: AIDS

CDC Centers for Disease Control and Prevention. HIV surveillance ---United States, 1981—2008. *Morbidity and Mortality Weekly Report (MMWR),* 11/16/2011. http://www.cdc.gov/mmwr/preview/mmwrhtml/mm60221a2.htm.

Barbo, B. (Speaker). (1989). *AIDS Related Death* (Cassette Recording). Hutchinson, Kansas: Regional Conference, The Compassionate Friends.

Chapter XXI: The Choking Game & Auto-Erotic Asphyxiation

1. Maxwell, L. A. (2008). CDC Tallies Toll from "Choking Game". *Education Week, 27.*

2. Ullrich, N. J., Bergin, A. M, & Goodkin, H. P. (2008). "The choking game": self-induced hypoxia presenting as recurrent seizure-like events. *Epilepsy & Behavior, 12.* 486-488.

3.   Andrew, T. A., & Fallon, K. K. (2007). Asphyxial games in children and adolescents. *American Journal of Forensic Medicine and Pathology. 28.* pp. 303-307.

4.   Brausch, A. M., Decker, K. M., & Hadley, A. G. (August, 2011). Risk of suicidal ideation in adolescents with both self-asphyxial risk-taking behavior and non-suicidal self-injury. *Suicide and Life Threatening Behavior, 41.*

Chapter XXII: A Mother's Plight: "How Did My Son Die:"

**Chapter XXIII: Every Exit is also an Entrance
    "Parable of the Twins"**

Acknowledgements:

This book would not have been possible without The Compassionate Friends and Alive Alone participants who filled out anonymous surveys. These valiant individuals poured out their hearts on paper, letting us all know we're not alone in our pain.

In the *Homicide Chapter*, four brave and strong individuals, Steve, Kim, Jo Ann and Jim, all told their stories of a horrible loss and much love in the hopes that it will help others. Obviously, this chapter would not have been possible without these four.

Likewise, Shawn told the heart-wrenching story of finding her son's body but never knowing how he died. Not knowing adds another whole dimension to grief. Thank you, Shawn, for sharing your story in *A Mother's Plight: How Did My Son Die?*

Amy told about her husband's fast downward spiral into drug addiction, his suicide one year later, and her desperate struggles with anxiety and PTSD (*Fear* and *Suicide Chapters*). Her mother, Shirley, also contributed much to this story. Thank you, my friends.

Tanya, in the *SIDS Chapter*, tells a grandmother's terrifying story about the SIDS death of her precious grandchild, "Little Lil." Tanya experienced another great loss one year later when her son, Darin, killed himself because he could not overcome the terrible guilt associated with SIDS.

Many of my friends contributed to various chapters with bits and pieces of their own tragedies. Thank you Judy, Sheri, Sue, Linda, Andy, Jen's mom and Jacob's mom. Thank you, Kay, for advising me.

A Big **Thank You** also goes to the following:

Two tireless ladies in the Abilene University Libraries spent countless hours looking up research articles and books for the various chapters in my book: Karen Hendrick, M.L.S., Abilene Christian University, and Leta Tillman, M.L.S., Hardin Simmons University. I'm anything but a "computer whiz", so they showed *extraordinary patience* when helping me.

My wonderful readers and editors made much needed corrections and suggestions – often to my chagrin. Chasley Dotson, M.S., Bonnie Campbell, M.S., Jo Ann Starkey and Francis Johnson all spent countless hours making suggestions and cleaning up faulty grammar and punctuations. My final editor, Sherry York, critiqued my work and is responsible for a much more reader-friendly book. I was hard-headed enough not to always take her suggestions; plus I continued to make changes to the manuscript, so blame only me for mistakes. I hate to take credit, but all mistakes are my doing.

Jim, thank you for the many hours you spent listening, reading and talking through problem areas with me.

My brother and sister-in-law (Sonny and Sue Sweet) made invaluable suggestions. Sonny was good at adding humor in places and letting his little sis know that she needed to do considerably more "whittling" on her manuscript.

The drawings in the Homicide Chapter are by Mike Jones, Director of Art at Hardin Simmons University. Thank you, Mike.

This book would not be were it not for Sangeeta Singg, Ph.D., my advisor and mentor. She is the person (besides my son Joe) who is most responsible for this book. She has always had faith in me.

And last, thank you Tarra, my friend, for believing in me and especially for *being there for me* after Joe's death.

Permissions:

My Compassionate Friends have been most helpful and supportive. **Iris Bolton**, whose workshops were so helpful to me in my early grief, not only gave permission for my extensive use of her quotes, but also sent me another copy of her book, *My Son, My Son,* a book about her son's suicide.

Likewise, **Beverly Barbo** sent a copy of her book, *The Walking Wounded* ©, her story about her son's homosexuality and AIDS related death. I used her quotes extensively in the AIDS chapter.

Margaret Gerner graciously gave her permission to use her quotes. *The Myth of Perfect Parenthood* article in my "Guilt" chapter and her portrayal of a "teapot about to blow" in my "Anger" chapter. Both so accurately represent our feelings at certain times. I thank you, Margaret.

Roberta Roper, veteran crime victim advocate, gave her approval to use her remarks regarding homicide victims in my "Homicide Chapter." Her daughter, Stephanie, not only had been raped and murdered, but she was further victimized by the court system.

Darcie Sims' workshops have been a great help and inspiration to me since the death of my son, Joe. Darcie not only gave permission to use her quote, but also gave me encouragement for my book.

Ashleigh Brilliant lovingly gave permission to use her poem in my "Finding Happiness Again" chapter. Her poem certainly struck a chord within me; the chapter would not be complete without it.

Therese A. Rando, Ph.D. gave her permission to quote (extensively) from her book, *Parental Loss of a Child ©*. This has been one of the most helpful books I have read, and I recommend it to all bereaved parents.

Pat Dyson's poem, *My Hero*, seemed perfect for my "Mothers and Fathers" chapter. Thank you, Pat.

Had I not attended Barbara Allen's workshops on Drug Related Deaths, I would have been much less knowledgeable about that topic. She was also the inspiration for *Story of the Two Arrows* that closes the chapter.

Article & Quote Permissions:

The Station Essay Team said they "would be honored" for me to mention The Station by Robert J. Hastings in my "Finding Happiness Again" chapter.

John T. Maltsberger, MD gave permission to use his quote about "suffering so great that it can drive people to suicide". ("Suicide Chapter")

The Andrews McMeel Publishing, LLC, gave permission to use Erma Bombeck's quote in my "Gifts from our Child" chapter.

Permission for the Zig Ziglar quote in the "Mothers and Fathers" chapter" was gladly given by Cindy Ziglar Oates, Customer Service Manager for Zig Ziglar.

Book Permissions:

You and Your Adolescent by Laurence Steinberg, Ph.D: Reprinted with the permission of Simon & Schuster Publishing Group. New and Revised Edition by Laurence Steinberg, Ph.D. Copyright ©1990, 1997 Laurence Steinberg and Ann Levine. Copyright © 2011 Laurence Steinberg, Ph.D.

On Children and Death by Elisabeth Kubler-Ross, M.D.:

Song Permissions:

Alan Pedersen gave his permission (to Steve Roberts) to use his song, *I'll Always Be Your Dad* ©. After losing his daughter, Ashley, age 18, he has been a true inspiration to other hurting parents through his music. Now, he is Executive Director of The Compassionate Friends.